Force

The biomechanics of training

Dr Dan Cleather

KMA Press

Prague, Czech Republic

ISBN-13: 9798467935775

For Kuba, Max and Alex

CONTENTS

ACKNOWLEDGMENTS

Thanks to Jon Goodwin for the careful critical reading and for being awesome. I feel like much of this book is my reinterpretation of his and Dan John's ideas. Of course, where I have made mistakes, the errors are all mine. Thanks also to Kat Daniels for some fun Twitter discussions and for giving comments on Chapter 26, to Peter Weyand for his permission to use the images in Figure 19 and to Stuart McMillan for providing the image in Figure 20.

This book was started before Covid, barely touched for most of the pandemic, but then completed during a period of self-isolation due to (asymptomatic) Covid infection. One surprising positive of Covid has been the opportunity to make real online friends. I am immensely grateful to have met Sophia Nimphius and Joseph Esformes, kindred spirits to me, who have been a source of inspiration and support.

Thanks to Hayley Legg for ALWAYS being there. Thanks also to Gill McInnes for making me feel valued and Stephen Patterson for his patience and wisdom.

Bara, když my se vzali, říkal jsem že nikdy jsem nevěřil že někdo by mi znal tak dobře. Ted', vice znáš můj duch. Kuba, Max and Alex, there is nothing that is even remotely as important to me as you are. I love you so much.

PREFACE

There are a lot of biomechanics books out there. Some are good and some are bad. Often whether a book is good or bad will depend on the reader and what they hope to learn from the book. For many practitioners (strength and conditioning coaches, personal trainers, physiotherapists, athletic trainers, etc), the most interesting part of a biomechanics book will be examples that show the practical relevance of the material. However, as far as I have seen, all biomechanics books share a similar logic in terms of their narrative direction. That is, the order of the books is dictated by the mathematical content and they are arranged in the most logical order for learning the mechanics. This is fantastic if the ultimate goal is to learn about the maths, however it can relegate the practical interpretation of the material to a secondary role.

This is a very different type of biomechanics book because its narrative is structured around the training process. First and foremost, what I try to do here is explain the purpose of training from a biomechanical perspective. I only introduce mechanical concepts when I need them to elaborate on the story that I am telling. This means that the order of presentation of the mathematics is pretty non-standard, but hopefully means that the relevance and importance of mechanical principles for training is clearer and more explicit.

The book is structured as follows. The first seven chapters describe what we are trying to achieve when we train (from a biomechanical standpoint). This essentially boils down to producing as much force as possible in the sporting environment (or, more strictly, and as we will see in Chapter 3, as much impulse). Having determined the goal of training, in Chapters 8 and 9, I talk about the general factors that need to be considered in order to ensure that our training is effective in improving our ability to express force in a way that is relevant for our sport. This is often referred to as the specificity of training. Most of the rest of the book is then comprised of a discussion of the way in which force is expressed during movement, and the implications of this for the training process.

Biomechanics is a discipline which seems to be particularly susceptible to pseudoscience. One of my goals in this book is to try and explain why some popular 'biomechanical' theories may not be as rigorous as they might seem. These discussions are presented throughout the book, in places that seemed most logical to me.

My main motivation in writing this book is to demonstrate that an understanding of biomechanics is fundamental to effective training practices. However, the relevance of the science is not in finding a particular study that examined x or y training practice in order to say whether the method is worthwhile or not. Rather, a deep appreciation for the way in which the body produces force, and how this varies depending on the task in hand, is one of the key considerations in designing effective training programmes.

*"From understanding Jin [trained force], we can
achieve enlightenment"*

The Canon of Tai Chi Chuan (Tai Chi Chuan Ching),
Often attributed to Wang Zong-yue (late eighteenth century),

Translation by Dan Docherty,
Tai Chi Chuan: Decoding the Classics for the Modern Martial Artist

INTRODUCTION

What is the purpose of training?

It seems most appropriate to start a book about training by asking what we are trying to achieve when we train. At the most basic level this can probably be boiled down to two aims – we train in order to improve our performance level and to reduce the likelihood that we will get injured. How can an understanding of force help us to achieve these aims?

Sporting performance is often predicated upon our ability to either change our own motion or the motion of an external body. As we will see shortly in order to change the motion of a body we need to apply a force to it. Our ability to move ourselves or to move things is therefore highly dependent on our ability to express force. Consequently, whether we are aware of it or not, one of the main outcomes of our training is to increase or refine our force expression capabilities.

At the same time as we exert forces on our external environment, we also load our bones, muscles, tendons and ligaments with internal forces. This loading is an important stimulus for training adaptations. However, the

3

most common mechanism for musculoskeletal injury is that one or more of these tissues is exposed to too much force. This can be in the form of a one-off event where the force exceeds the load bearing capacity of the tissue (e.g. in the case of a bone break or muscle tear) or because the tissue is exposed to repeated loading over a period of time that exceeds the tissue's ability to adapt (as occurs in chronic overuse injuries). Thus, if we want to reduce the likelihood that we get injured, we need to understand the forces that our bodily structures experience during movement.

At the most fundamental level, sports performance can probably be reduced to just two dimensions – the actual physical performance capability of the athlete and then the athlete's ability to use these capacities within the competitive environment. To use an autosport analogy, we have the capabilities of the car, and the capabilities of the driver. In training we want to improve both. The capabilities of the 'driver' include things like the athlete's ability to read and predict what is happening in the competitive arena, to deceive opponents and to be able to compete effectively (which in turn encompasses their psychological make-up). The capacity of the 'car' can essentially be boiled down again to just two inter-related elements – that is, the abilities of the athlete to access energy and to express force. This book is principally about the latter ability, although we will also touch on the relationship between force expression and energy needs.

Lost in translation

Biomechanics is the application of mechanical principles to biological organisms. For the purpose of this book this will comprise the analysis of the forces acting on, and expressed by, an athlete. As we have just seen, such an analysis is fundamental to the understanding of athletic performance. However, despite the importance of a clear understanding of force, it is very common for coaches to make mistakes in the interpretation of some of the most basic biomechanical principles. Why is this?

The problem arises because some of the technical terms used in mechanics overlap with some everyday language. In particular, in mechanics we talk about force, work and power, and these terms all have strict mechanical and mathematical definitions. Unfortunately, the way that we use these words in everyday language often does not correspond with the mechanical definition. For instance, in mechanics, power is 'the rate of doing work'. However, a dictionary definition of power might be something like 'the capability to act in a particular way', 'the ability to influence the behaviour of someone else', or 'physical strength or the force expressed by something'*. The dictionary definitions are clearly both very different and much wider than the mechanical definition. To add to the confusion, the latter dictionary definition actually equates power with another mechanical quantity, force – suggesting that power and force are the same thing.

It is thus really easy for the uninitiated to get confused. It is entirely natural to read a word like 'power' in a biomechanical text and to understand this in terms of one of the dictionary definitions. However, this can quickly lead to a fundamental misunderstanding of the biomechanics.

At the outset of this book it is thus vital that we recognise that words like force or power have both an everyday and a mechanical meaning. Many people don't realise this, and this is a constant source of misunderstanding. It is also imperative that when we talk about biomechanics we are vigilant about using terminology precisely. It is really easy to slip and to use mechanical terminology according to the common vernacular – especially when trying to convince the lay person.

Throughout this book I will try to outline some of the common mistakes that people make in applying biomechanics to questions of training. In many cases these problems are simply a result of imprecision in terminology. To a large part then, this book is about having clarity in the meaning of biomechanical terms, and then deriving training insights from them.

---

* Dictionary definitions paraphrased from the Oxford English Dictionary.

1 ARISTOTLE VERSUS NEWTON

What is a force?

Trying to answer the question 'What is a force?' is very far from being a trivial task. It is true that most of us have some intuitive understanding of what a force 'is'. However, when we are actually asked to define a force we discover that something we thought we understood is actually pretty difficult to pin down. Many of us would probably settle on the somewhat vague definition that a force is a push or a pull, but would have the nagging suspicion that our explanation was missing something.

The reason for our difficulty is that a force is not something we can see. In fact, some philosophers of science would argue that a force is not something that even really exists at all. Instead, force is our attempt to explain the causes of motion (or actually, the causes of a change in motion, but we will come to this shortly). We actually define force in terms of the effects it has on motion. For instance, we know that if we push something it will start moving, and if we push it harder it will move faster. Force thus describes a quality of the push – how hard it is, or more strictly, its tendency to create changes in motion.

Given that we define a force based upon its effect, we could argue that a force is not a "thing" per se, but rather a concept or theoretical construct. If this is the case, force is also a pretty nebulous concept. We use it to describe the changes in motion caused by actual physical, material interactions between objects – our pushes and pulls*. However, we also talk about forces that exist in the absence of motion. Similarly, we use the same concept to describe the mutual attraction that exists between massive bodies (gravity) or the repulsion/attraction between charged bodies (electromagnetism).

To summarise, defining the meaning of force is not simple...

Our intuition is stuck in Ancient Greece

So we have decided that we will define a force by reference to its effects. Unfortunately, the next problem that we encounter is that determining the effects of a force is also non-trivial. We might be inclined to think that our common sense will tell us what happens when we push, pull or drop something, however frequently it can lead us astray. For instance, our intuition tells us that if we drop two similarly sized balls of differing weights from a tall tower that the heavier ball will hit the ground first (when in actual fact they will make contact with the ground at the same time). We shouldn't feel too bad if we make this mistake however – no less a thinker than Aristotle thought exactly the same thing.

Aristotle devoted considerable effort to the problem of motion. In particular, he observed (as did we on the previous page) that if we push

---

* Dr Kat Daniels (@KAJDaniels) described a force to me as being the consequence of an interaction. I also like this as an alternative definition, which as we will see, emerges from Newton's 3rd Law.

something it will start moving and if we push it harder it will go faster*. Similarly, he noted that in order to keep the object moving we need to keep pushing it. He explained this by suggesting that the application of a force is the cause of an object's velocity (speed). That is, force (*F*) is directly proportional to velocity (*v*), or:

$$F \propto v$$

Some variation of this law remained the dominant definition of force for around the next 2000 years. Even today, our intuition will tell us the same thing, and for exactly the same reasons as Aristotle – that is, we tend to feel that things will only move if we are pushing them.

Newton's 1st Law

Isaac Newton revolutionised our understanding of the causes of movement with his eponymous three laws. We can best understand this by contrasting his laws with the Aristotelian position. Let's consider his 1st Law.

---

* Speed is how quickly we cover a particular distance. For instance, if it is **d** metres from point A to point B, and it takes us **t** seconds to get from A to B, then our speed (**s**) is given by:

$$s = \frac{d}{t}$$

Speed is the rate of change of distance, i.e. it tells us how many metres we cover each second (ms^{-1}). Speed is a scalar quality – it tells us how fast we are moving but not the direction of travel.

Velocity is how quickly we change our location. If we talk about a change in location we need to specify both the distance moved and the direction. Thus velocity is vector quality – it has magnitude and direction. In the previous example, if point B lay directly east of A then our velocity would be **s** ms^{-1} in an easterly direction.

"Every body perseveres in its state of being at rest or of moving uniformly straight forward, unless it is compelled to change its state by application of a force."

The first part of this law is the same as for Aristotle – things that are still, will only start moving if we push them. However the second part is entirely different – it says that if something is moving it will continue moving with the same speed and in the same direction unless we push it. This is diametrically opposite to our intuitive sense that we need to keep pushing something if it is to continue moving. So how has our intuition failed us? Well arguably it hasn't – in our everyday experience if we start a wheel rolling or throw a ball they don't keep moving, but instead come to a rest. What is important here is that the reason they stop moving is because there is a force acting on them that changes their motion, be it wind resistance, friction or gravity. If the object was moving in outer space and thus not subject to any forces, it would keep moving indefinitely.

Newton's 2nd Law

Newton's 2nd Law is one of the most well-known laws of nature and it to all intents and purposes provides us with the modern definition of force.

"The rate of change in motion is proportional to the force applied and takes place along the straight line in which that force is impressed."

'A change in motion' means a change in the velocity of the object. The rate of change of velocity of an object is its acceleration*, thus Newton's 2nd Law defines force as being proportional to acceleration (a).

---

* Acceleration is how quickly our velocity is changing, i.e. by how much our velocity changes each second. It is calculated by dividing the change in velocity by the time taken for that change.

$$a = \frac{\text{change in } v}{\text{change in t}} = \frac{\Delta v}{\Delta t}$$

$$F \propto a$$

Clearly this is also very different to the ideas of Aristotle. Newton proposed that rather than force being the cause of an object's velocity, rather it was the cause of the change in the object's velocity. The distinction is important and it is very common for people to miss its significance. For instance, you will often hear the claim that forces are the cause of motion – they are not, they are the cause of changes in motion.

Newton's 2nd Law is probably best known as the relationship between force, mass (m) and acceleration.

$$F = ma$$

That is, the force required in order to achieve a given acceleration is also proportional to the mass of the object.

Newton's 3rd Law

> *"To any action there is always an opposite and equal reaction; in other words the actions of the two bodies upon each other are always equal and always opposite in direction."*

As my good friend Jon Goodwin is want to say, if we push on something, it will push back – even if it doesn't have muscles. This effect is often highly important in sport – in many movements we push into the ground, and the ground pushes back on us. This 'ground reaction force' is the force that actually changes our motion. For instance, during vertical jumping it is the ground reaction force that propels us into the air.

The calculation of velocity is analogous to that of acceleration. If x is our location:

$$v = \frac{\text{change in } x}{\text{change in } t} = \frac{\Delta x}{\Delta t}$$

A note on Einstein

It should be noted that Newtonian mechanics does not represent the cutting edge of modern physics. Rather, Einstein in turn revolutionised physics with his theories of special and general relativity. In actual fact, Newton's laws just describe a special case of Einstein's universe where the observer and all objects are within the same inertial frame. Thankfully, our movements in sport and training are an example of this special case, and thus we can restrict our biomechanical analyses to Newtonian (classical) mechanics.

Retraining our intuition

In the introduction we have already seen that the understanding of mechanics is complicated by the fact that many mechanical terms also have an informal popular meaning that is different from their mechanical definition. What this chapter has shown is that in addition we sometimes cannot rely on our first instincts in order to understand the effect of forces, as our intuition can be misleading. The process of becoming an excellent coach therefore also involves the retraining of our intuition such that we see the sporting world through Newton's eyes.

2 CHANGING VELOCITY

Force? Who cares?

So where are we? We have managed to define force and have some rules which describe what forces do. However, we seem to be proceeding in a backwards fashion – we haven't yet talked about what we are trying to achieve with our biomechanical analysis, why we need to understand force, or why this is relevant to sport and training. Let's do this now...

Ultimately, very often one of the key factors in sports performance is the ability of the athlete to change their velocity or the velocity of an external object. Running, acceleration, jumping, throwing, lifting, striking and changing direction all involve a change in velocity, for instance:

- How high we jump is entirely dependent on our velocity at the point we leave the ground;

- How far we throw is largely dependent on the velocity of the implement at the point of release;

- Change of direction (e.g. cutting) requires the athlete to decelerate their motion in the direction of travel, and then re-accelerate in a new direction.

Now forces cause changes in velocity, hence our interest in them.

Rate versus magnitude of change

It is important to realise that in sport we are often most interested in the magnitude of the change of velocity during the course of a particular movement. For instance, in a vertical jump we might start from a stationary standing position. As we have seen, how high we jump is entirely dependent on our take-off velocity. Thus the critical performance variable is how much we increase (change) our velocity. If we are simply interested in jumping as high as we can, we don't mind if it takes us longer to achieve this change in velocity if the end result is a greater change.

Newton's 2nd Law provides us with a relationship between the force applied and the acceleration experienced by an object. However, acceleration is the rate of change of velocity. It is critical that we understand that this is an instantaneous relationship – it just tells us how quickly velocity is changing in one particular moment. This doesn't tell us what was the overall change in velocity over the movement.

Of course, if the acceleration over the duration of the movement is constant (i.e. the force applied is constant) then it is simple to work out the change in velocity: We know that:

$$a = \frac{\Delta v}{\Delta t}$$

And so:

$$\Delta v = a \times \Delta t = \frac{F}{m} \times \Delta t$$

Human movement isn't constantly accelerated

Unfortunately human movement isn't generally constantly accelerated. For instance, it takes us time to generate force and the amount of force that we can apply is highly dependent on the posture of our body at any given moment. The variable nature of force expression is illustrated by the force-time graphs for some common human movements that are depicted in Figure 1.

Figure 1. Force-time graphs for some common human movements (note that axes are not to scale relative to one another).

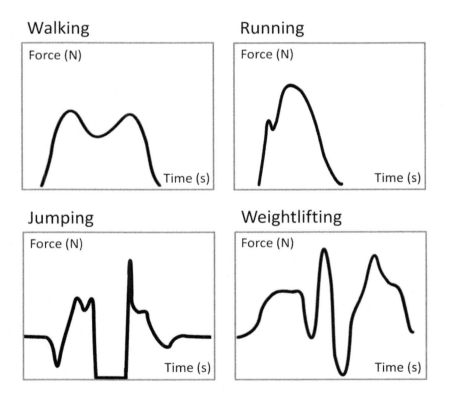

It is clear that the force-time relationship in all of these movements is highly non-linear and certainly not constant. This means that we can't simply calculate the change in velocity using the previous equation. How can we possibly work out the change in velocity during these movements?

3 HOW MUCH FORCE?

What variable?

Let's approach the problem of finding the change in velocity from a different angle. We know, from Newton's 2nd Law, that forces are the cause of changes in velocity. Therefore, if more force is applied during a movement then the change in velocity must be greater. But how can we say 'how much' force has been applied? How do we calculate the 'total force' applied during the movement? To put this in terms of the force-time curves we saw in Figure 1, we have a highly non-linear curve that represents the force applied over the course of the movement. What aspect of the curve would best express if a lot of force was applied or not?

One reasonable solution might be to look at the maximum force that was achieved. However, this will just tell us how much force there was at one instant in time – this doesn't mean that force was necessarily high over the whole period. To get a better idea of the force that was applied over the whole movement we could calculate the average force that was applied. However, this in turn doesn't tell us anything about the duration of the force application – and longer force application surely means 'more' total force.

Impulse

Instead, let's consider calculating the area underneath the force-time curve. There will be more area under the curve if the peak force is higher, if the average force was greater, or if force was applied for longer. Thus the area under the curve seems like a good choice for quantifying how much force was applied as it will capture the different ways in which we can apply more force. We give the area underneath the force-time curve a special name – impulse (I). However, it might be easier to understand if you think of impulse as 'total force'.

Impulse-momentum relationship

As we might expect given that forces are the cause of changes in velocity, there is a direct relationship between impulse applied and the change in velocity. More impulse, i.e. more total force, means that there will be a greater change in velocity. In fact, impulse and change in velocity are directly proportional to each other:

$$I \propto \Delta v$$

More strictly, the impulse applied is equal to the change in momentum (momentum is mass multiplied by velocity):

$$I = m \times \Delta v$$

We can rearrange this equation to find the change in velocity:

$$\Delta v = \frac{I}{m}$$

For those that are interested, the derivation of the impulse-momentum relationship can be found in this footnote*.

---

* This relationship can be derived directly from Newton's 2nd Law. Let's say I wanted to calculate the area under this curve:

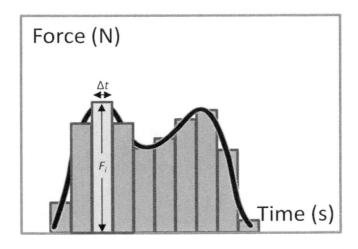

I could do so by dividing the area into rectangles of equal width (Δt) as shown, calculating the area of each rectangle and then adding all the areas together. Now the area of the lighter shaded rectangle (call it rectangle i) is:

$$I_i = F_i \times \Delta t$$

But from Newton's 2nd Law we know that:

$$F_i = ma_i$$

And the acceleration during this period is the change in velocity divided by the change in time:

$$a_i = \frac{\Delta v_i}{\Delta t}$$

Combining these two equations gives us:

Impulse, impulse, impulse

We have already seen that our change in velocity during a movement is often a critical performance variable. We have now shown that the cause of our change in velocity is the impulse that we apply. This means that in many cases we can explain differences in explosive physical performances in terms of impulse generation. Impulse will often be the most important performance variable. I'll say that again, impulse will often be the most important performance variable. However, in coaching and training circles it is rare for there to be much, if any, focus on impulse. Instead, coaches tend to be more interested in other variables like peak power or peak force.

$$F_i = m\frac{\Delta v_i}{\Delta t}$$

Now multiply both sides of this equation by the change in time:

$$F_i \times \Delta t = m\frac{\Delta v_i}{\Delta t} \times \Delta t$$

The Δt's on the right hand side of the equation cancel each other out so we have:

$$F_i \times \Delta t = m \times \Delta v_i$$

The left hand side of this equation is the formula for the area of the rectangle or the impulse, so we have:

$$I_i = m \times \Delta v_i$$

That is, the impulse of the lighter shaded rectangle i is equal to the change in momentum over that time period. Now in order to calculate the total impulse, we add up all of the rectangles (let's say there are n of them):

$$I_1 + \cdots + I_i + \cdots + I_n = m \times \Delta v_1 + \cdots + m \times \Delta v_i + \cdots + m \times \Delta v_n$$

So the total impulse is equal to the total change in momentum:

$$I = m \times \Delta v$$

This is not a force-velocity relationship

One of the most common errors in biomechanics, is to think that the impulse-momentum relationship is effectively a force-velocity relationship. Remember that intuitively, like Aristotle, we have a tendency to 'feel' that force should be related to velocity – i.e. that more force should mean more velocity:

$$F \propto v$$

The impulse-momentum relationship tells us that impulse or 'total force' is related to the change in velocity:

$$\text{'total' } F \propto \Delta v$$

Why isn't this the same as a force-velocity relationship? The critical point here is that there is no direct instantaneous relationship between the force and the velocity. That is, if we know the force at a particular time we still don't know the velocity of an object with a known mass – the force could be large, but the object be moving slowly, or vice versa. In contrast, Newton's 2nd Law defines an instantaneous relationship between force and acceleration. If we know the force acting on a known mass then we can directly calculate the acceleration of the object. If the force is large then so is the acceleration.

It is important to remember that the impulse-momentum relationship is about the magnitude (amount) of change in velocity over a particular period of time, whereas Newton's 2nd law is an instantaneous relationship reflecting the rate of change in that moment. The magnitude of change is independent of the actual velocity that the object is travelling at. If we apply a certain amount of impulse to an object then the increase in its velocity will be the same if it starts from rest or if it is travelling at 100 miles per hour.

4 MAXIMISING IMPULSE

How can we increase the impulse applied?

It is clear then, that for many sporting activities, in order to improve our performance we need to increase the amount of impulse that we apply during a movement. That is, we need to increase the area under the force-time curve. There are effectively three ways that we can do this.

Increase peak or average force

Probably the simplest way to increase the impulse applied (i.e. the 'total force') is simply to increase the magnitude of the force applied during a particular part of the movement. For instance, Figure 2 presents the force-time graph for the propulsive phase of a vertical jump. In the second panel we can see that if the peak force is increased, then the area underneath the curve is clearly increased as well. It is important to note here if the height of any part of the curve is increased that the area under the curve is increased – the increase doesn't have to be at the peak. Average force can thus be increased, increasing the impulse, with the peak force being unchanged.

Figure 2. Increasing impulse during vertical jumping. Top left panel indicates the original jump. The other three panels illustrate the increase in area under the curve with greater peak force, greater rate of force development (RFD) and a longer duration of force application.

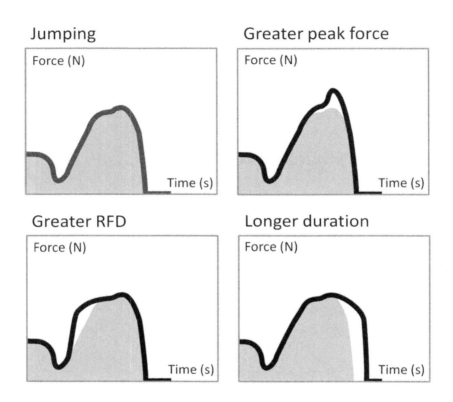

Increase rate of force development

An alternative strategy is to increase our rate of force development* (RFD; F'). If there is a greater RFD then the force-time curve will have a steeper

---

* Rate of force development is the rate of change of force with respect to time. It indicates how quickly the amount of force being applied is increasing. If we consider the force-time graph (on the next page), the rate of force development is the average gradient of the curve for the period under consideration.

gradient (as indicated in Figure 2). This means the athlete reaches near maximal force expression more quickly, resulting in a curve that is wider towards the top and hence has more area.

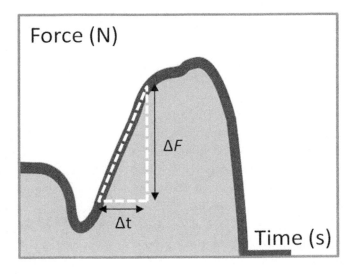

The gradient is as follows:

$$F' = \frac{\text{change in } F}{\text{change in t}} = \frac{\Delta F}{\Delta t}$$

In this book I will use F' (F-dash) as the symbol for rate of force development. The dash just indicates that it is the rate of change of F.

Often in training we talk about rate of force development over a particular time period – it is important that the time period is defined. Alternatively we can calculate the instantaneous rate of force development. This can be visualized by imagining the time period indicated on the diagram as vanishingly small – the rate of force development is the gradient of this tiny triangle (and is the tangent to the curve at the point of interest).

Increase the duration of force application

The final method to increase impulse is to increase the duration of the force application. Of course, in some skills this is neither possible nor desirable, as there is a limited time available for force application. For instance, in maximum speed sprinting the duration of each foot contact will typically be around 0.1s, and it would be detrimental to an athlete's performance to increase this. Thus, in order to maximise impulse production in sprinting the athlete will need to either improve their maximum force capabilities or their RFD. However, for movements where it is possible or desirable, increasing the time of force application clearly increases the impulse.

Trade-offs

The most appropriate way to maximise impulse application will depend on a range of different factors including the nature of the skill, competitive considerations, the environment and the characteristics of the athlete. What is important to realise is that all of the methods for increasing impulse can affect each other, and so an increase in one variable does not necessarily mean that there will be an overall increase in impulse. For instance, an athlete might increase their peak force production, but in doing so decrease the duration of the force application, and the overall effect of this could be to decrease impulse. This is one reason why measuring peak force, average force or RFD is inferior to the measurement of impulse.

A study of jump technique and impulse

In order to put these considerations into practical terms let's try to explain why vertical jump technique varies in different sports and different environments. Remember that how high we jump is entirely dependent on how much impulse we impress, and so optimal jump technique will facilitate the greatest expression of impulse within the constraints of the competitive environment.

First of all, it is interesting to note that the gross movement strategy that humans adopt in vertical jumping is highly consistent. In particular, when people jump they exhibit a proximal to distal* pattern of joint extension – i.e. the hip starts to extend first, followed by the knee and then the ankle. One reason for this pattern is to prolong the amount of time that the athlete is in contact with the floor to allow more impulse to be impressed. The arms are used in a similar way – if we swing our arms upwards at the start of the propulsive phase this actually presses our body down into the floor (as a result of Newton's 3rd Law). The floor then has to press back on us (also due to Newton's 3rd Law) increasing the ground reaction force. This will also tend to give us more time in which to develop force.

Better jumpers, by definition, are able to impress more impulse during jumping. Of course, this can be achieved simply by having the ability to express high forces in short time periods. However, skilful jumpers are also able to coordinate the extension of their lower limb in order to maximise impulse expression. For instance, skilful jumpers gain more benefit from using their arms than novices – they are able to remain in contact with the ground for longer, or to sustain the period of higher force expression for longer.

The way in which we jump is influenced by the rules of the sport that we are playing. In some sports, the most important variable is simply how high we jump, and it doesn't matter how long we take to get off the floor. For instance, an outside hitter in volleyball is able to predict where and when the set will arrive and thus generally has lots of time available to jump. In these situations it is common for an athlete to adopt a 'hip dominant' strategy – that is, they will have a more inclined trunk with more hip flexion. This is a slower jumping strategy which can facilitate the production of more impulse. In contrast, in some sports the time available to jump is limited. For example, in basketball the athlete who snags a rebound is the one who reaches a certain height first. In these situations it is

---

* Proximal means closer to the centre of the body (the torso). Distal means further from the centre of the body.

more common to see a "knee dominant" jumping strategy, where the athlete remains more upright.

Similarly, the surface that an athlete competes on can also influence jump technique. Let's compare jumping to block in volleyball and beach volleyball. In beach volleyball, athletes will tend to squat much (much) deeper in the countermovement of their jump. This makes the propulsive phase longer allowing the athlete to generate more impulse. Why don't indoor volleyball players use this strategy then? The critical difference is the sand – it is hard to push off sand which will yield to pressure from the feet. This makes it hard to exert high forces and so players compensate for this by making their jump last longer. In contrast, indoors volleyball players can generate much higher peak forces by keeping their lower limb relatively more stiff and showing a greater degree of 'bounce' off the floor. The optimal strategy here is then to produce higher forces by sacrificing jump duration (it should be noted that there is also a competitive advantage to jumping quicker, and that given the nature of the two sports this is more important indoors).

Hopefully this brief analysis illustrates how important an understanding of impulse is in interpreting sport. This information is critical for informing training. For instance, beach and indoor volleyball players use completely different strategies for jumping and their training should differ accordingly.

5 VELOCITY-BASED TRAINING

Measuring stuff

Biomechanics is fundamental to understanding sport and training. However, for many coaches, the main time when they explicitly engage with biomechanical questions is in thinking about how they test their athlete's performance. There are broadly two main purposes to performance testing. The first is to try and quantify training induced increases in an athlete's performance capability. The second is to monitor and adjust training sessions based on the athlete's current physical state.

There are a wide variety of different variables that can be measured when we come to performance test our athletes. Some popular variables include force, power, time, load and velocity. Equally, for any particular variable there are a range of options – for instance, do we look at peak force or average force. In choosing exactly what we want to measure it is most appropriate to consider what variable is most meaningful in influencing performance. From the discussion that we have seen in the previous couple of chapters, in many cases this variable might be impulse, or one of the variables that influences the amount of impulse impressed (RFD, peak force, average force). Despite this, impulse is not the most common choice (at least in the weight room). Instead, power and velocity are probably the most popular performance measures. In this chapter we will consider the measurement of velocity and why it may be appropriate and then in the next chapter we will take an in depth look at power.

How do we measure impulse?

If we want to quantify impulse then we need to measure the force expression over time. In sport and training, the most common way to achieve this is through the use of a force plate – a piece of equipment that can be considered to be a glorified bathroom scale. In recent years, the cost of force plates has been decreasing and there are now a number of user-friendly force plates on the market that are designed for use by coaches. However, despite this there are still some barriers to their use – in particular that they still tend to be quite bulky and so are not the most portable tools.

An alternative method by which we can (indirectly) measure force is to use an accelerometer. As the name suggests, accelerometers give a measure of the acceleration which they are experiencing. From Newton's 2nd Law we know that acceleration is proportional to force, and in particular, if we know the mass of the body that is accelerating we can then determine the force. Thus it is theoretically possible to back out force-time data from acceleration-time data. The advantage of accelerometers is that they are small and portable and can thus be easily incorporated within wearable technology.

What has all this got to do with velocity?

Somewhat strangely, many commercial devices that are used to monitor resistance training and that incorporate accelerometers don't actually output acceleration or force. Instead, it is common for such devices to provide data relating to the velocity of the movement – for instance, mean or peak velocity. Generally, higher velocities are then considered to be desirable, and the velocity with which an athlete executes a movement is then used to inform training decisions.

At first glance then, the use of accelerometers in contemporary practice seems to run contrary to the analysis that prefaced this chapter. Why are we reporting velocity if the most interesting variable is impulse? I think the answer to this is probably quite mundane – the concept of velocity based training is intuitively easy for coaches and athletes to understand and accept, and there is now an established tradition of practising in this way. However, if we dig a little deeper, the use of velocity is probably not unreasonable.

Let's consider using peak velocity as a variable to quantify training. We know that there is a direct relationship between change in velocity and impulse. We also know that the athlete will generally be starting a repetition of a resistance training exercise from rest. Our peak velocity measurement is thus also the change in velocity over the movement up to the point of peak velocity. From the impulse-momentum relationship this will be directly proportional to the impulse impressed during this time period. Peak velocity is therefore a pretty good proxy for the impulse impressed during the main propulsive phase of the movement. In addition, it is easy to understand, and although the nature of the performance is described by only one number, we do get a picture of what happened over the duration of the main propulsive phase*. The disadvantage is that we don't get the richer information which would be provided by the whole force-time curve – that is, exactly how was the impulse generated.

This is not a force-velocity relationship!

So, as far as I can see, the main rationale for using velocity to guide training, rather than the acceleration (or force), which is directly measured by an accelerometer, is that it is easier to understand. However, this might also add to the confusion around the relationship between force and velocity. In particular, it gives athletes and coaches another opportunity to conflate

---

* This is a touch counterintuitive and is worth elaborating on. Peak velocity is an instantaneous measure – it just describes the motion of the body in one instant. However, because we know that we started from rest, we are able to infer the 'total' force applied over the phase too.

change in velocity with instantaneous velocity or 'total' force (impulse) with force.

6 POWER: WHO CARES?

The influence of terminology

Most coaches want their athletes to be powerful. In expressing this desire the term 'powerful' has its common every day meaning – it is not used in the strict mechanical sense. What do coaches mean by powerful? This will vary, but probably encompasses things like being 'explosive', being strong and fast, being able to accelerate themselves or external objects rapidly, etc... How might we define these qualities in mechanical terms? Well, they can all probably be described by some aspect of the force-time curve – the RFD, peak or average force, or impulse.

However, rather than being focussed on the force production capabilities of their athletes, many coaches are obsessed by their power output capabilities. This is understandable, but is based on a faulty understanding of the mechanics. Coaches want powerful athletes and so it seems logical to measure power output. However, the common meaning of 'powerful' in everyday language is not the same as 'power' in the strict mechanical sense. A confusion over terminology is leading these coaches to focus on a less relevant variable.

How much force revisited?

In Chapter 3 we asked how we could measure the 'total' force expressed during a movement. Our answer to this was to use the area under the force-time curve – the impulse. However there is another common way to calculate total force. Figure 3 presents the force-time curve and the position-time curve during vertical jumping. By combining these two curves we can plot a force-position curve as shown in the right hand panel of Figure 3 (note that in this case the position is the height of the centre of mass). So now, instead of depicting the force at each moment in time, we are depicting the force at each position the athlete is in. Similarly, rather than summing the force 'over time' as we did to calculate the impulse, we can instead sum the force 'over position'. That is, we calculate the area underneath the force-position curve.

Figure 3. Height-time, force-time and force-height curves for a typical vertical jump.

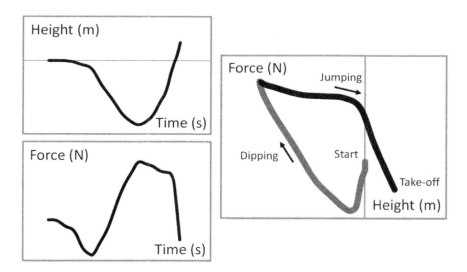

The area underneath the force-position curve is called the work. It is the 'total' force with respect to the distance moved. Note that to be more precise about our description of impulse, we should say it is the 'total' force with respect to the time taken.

Positive and negative work

There is a little wrinkle with regards to the calculation of work. Whereas time only moves forwards, our position can move both backwards and forwards. This won't have escaped your attention – it is why the force-height curve in Figure 3 has such a peculiar shape. The jump starts at the point indicated on the graph, and then the height of the centre of mass decreases as the athlete dips during the countermovement of the jump. The downward motion is represented by the grey line. At the end of the countermovement the athlete then begins to move upwards – this part of the movement is represented by the black line.

During the dipping phase, the direction in which the athlete is moving (downwards) is opposite to the direction of the force (upwards). The work done is thus negative. During the propulsive phase of the jump, the direction of travel and the direction of the force are the same (upwards) and thus the work done is positive. The net work done during the movement is therefore the positive work minus the negative work – that is, the area underneath the black line minus the area underneath the grey line.

What has all this got to do with power?

Power is defined to be the rate of doing work. That is, power is the amount of work done in a particular period of time. What does this look like? In Figure 4, I have added markers to our force-position curve at 40ms intervals. It is clear that these markers aren't evenly spaced. This is because the athlete's velocity varies over the course of the movement, and thus in some periods they cover more distance than in others.

Figure 4. Force-height curve during vertical jumping. Circles indicate 40ms intervals.

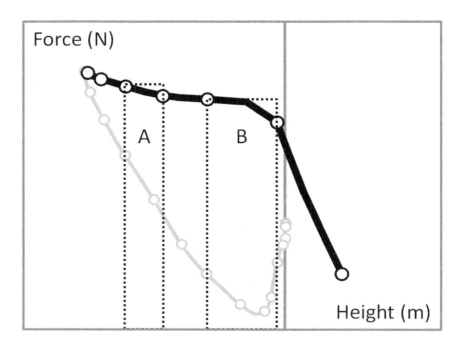

Now compare the rectangles labelled A and B, that approximate the area under the curve (work done), for these two time periods. It is obviously apparent that more work was done in the period labelled B, and thus the average power output during this period was also higher.

As power (P) is the rate of doing work (W) it can be calculated as follows:

$$P = \frac{\Delta W}{\Delta t}$$

But I thought that power was force times velocity

Well yes, but not by definition... A brief derivation of this is given in the footnote*, but yes, instantaneous power can be calculated in this way.

$$P = F.v$$

This is all a bit complicated isn't it?

Err, kind of, yes…

My motivation for showing what power is in such detail, other than to promote understanding, is to show that the mechanical meaning of power isn't as intuitive as the word seems to suggest. Of course, this doesn't necessarily mean that the variable isn't interesting, and if there was some

---

* In order to understand this consider Figure 4. Work done is the area under the curve. We can calculate this by dividing the curve into a series of rectangles, and then working out the area of the rectangles, in a similar way as we did in Chapter 3 for impulse. Now for a given rectangle, i:

$$\Delta W_i = F_i \times \Delta x_i$$

Now the rate of change of work, is the change in work, divided by the time taken. So if we divide both sides of this equation by the change in time we get:

$$\frac{\Delta W_i}{\Delta t} = F_i \times \frac{\Delta x_i}{\Delta t}$$

But:

$$v = \frac{\Delta x}{\Delta t}$$

And so we have:

$$P_i = F_i \times v_i$$

type of direct link with performance this would justify our interest in power, despite the complexity.

Remember that in Chapter 2 we saw that for many explosive sports skills that the change in velocity during the movement is often one of the most important performance variables. This is why impulse is so important for us – impulse accrued is directly proportional to the velocity change. Unfortunately, there isn't the same type of direct link between power and change in velocity and so it is less useful for quantifying explosive sports performance (there is a direct link for endurance performance that we will look at in a later chapter).

There is however an indirect link between power and change in velocity. This means that power will still tend to be well correlated with explosive performances like vertical jumping or weightlifting. These correlations lead coaches to believe that power is the most important variable and are sometimes used to justify their interest in it.

Peak power output: Who cares?

The measurement of peak (i.e. instantaneous maximal) power output is very popular in training, however for many activities it may not be the most helpful variable to track. We have already explored the reasons why power output generally may not be the best choice of performance variable. However, considering power output at one single moment in time is possibly even more limited. Can a snapshot taken at a single moment in time represent the most important performance aspects of a movement?

Figure 5 presents the power-, force-, velocity- and height-time graphs for a typical vertical jump. The vertical line indicates the instant that peak power output occurs. What is clear is that this event is not coincident with any other key events in terms of the force, velocity or displacement of the athlete. Peak power output occurs just prior to the point that the athlete leaves the ground. At this point velocity is near, but just short of, maximal. At the same time, although force is relatively high, it is rapidly decreasing. The question is whether a focus on peak power output, and consequently a focus on the force production immediately prior to take-off, is the most meaningful. I would suggest that in many cases the answer to this question is no.

Figure 5. Power output, velocity, jump height and force for a typical vertical jump (all measures relative to time).

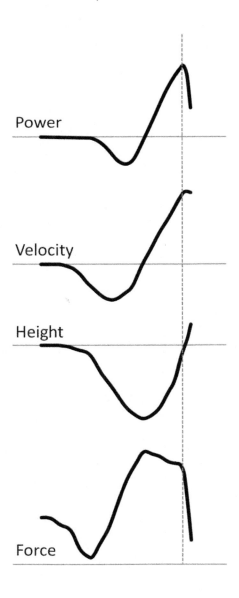

7 GRAVITY

A force of attraction?

So far our analysis has neglected a critical contributor to performance – gravity. But what is gravity? To be honest, no one really knows. In the same way that we defined forces in terms of the effects that they cause, gravity is our explanation for an effect that we can observe. In this case, the effect that we are talking about is the tendency of objects to be attracted to one another. This attraction is proportional to the masses of the objects. However, the cause of this attraction is not visible to us, despite the fact that we experience the effect every day of our lives.

The most sophisticated explanation for the effect of gravity is given by Einstein's theory of general relativity. According to this theory, the mass of an object distorts the fabric of space-time and gravity is a result of the undulating landscape of different sized troughs around each object. Don't worry though, such a complicated description of gravity is unnecessary for our purposes and again we can rely on Newton for our analysis.

Newton's model of gravitation was to represent the attraction between objects by a gravitational force. He proposed that this force is proportional to the product of the masses of the two objects (m_1 and m_2) and inversely proportional to the square of the distance (r) between them:

$$F = \frac{Gm_1m_2}{r^2}$$

Note that G is the gravitational constant.

Gravity is a weak "force", and the attraction between ourselves and the objects around us is tiny enough to be immaterial. However, the Earth itself is a very large object, and thus it exerts a relatively strong attractive force upon us. At the same time, we spend our whole lives at a relatively constant distance from the centre of the Earth. These two facts mean that for practical purposes we can describe the force of gravity that acts on an object on Earth by Newton's 2nd Law:

$$F = mg$$

In this equation, g is the acceleration due to gravity, which on the Earth's surface is $9.81ms^{-2}$ directed towards the centre of the Earth.

Weight

Our weight is the force that acts on us due to the attraction of our body mass to the Earth. Our weight is an important concern in any analysis of our movement. Even when we are standing at rest we need to exert a force on the ground that is equal to our weight to prevent ourselves being accelerated downwards. In movement it is important to understand that we are constantly subject to this force. If we want to propel ourselves away from the Earth we have to exert a force that is at least in excess of our weight.

Net impulse

In our earlier discussion of impulse we neglected the effect of gravity and the need to overcome our body weight when moving. Figure 6 illustrates the force-time graph for jumping and landing that we saw previously. However, this graph now includes a grey shaded area that represents the force (and impulse) that would be expressed if the athlete were simply standing still. This impulse does not contribute to the jump height achieved by the athlete. Instead, the propulsive impulse is the total impulse (area under the black line) net of the body weight impulse. We calculate this net impulse by subtracting the shaded grey area from the area under the force-time curve.

Figure 6. Force-time graph for jumping and landing. Grey area indicates body weight impulse.

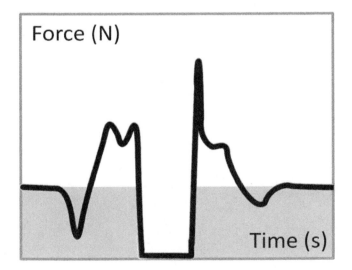

8 SPECIFICITY

What is the purpose of training (revisited)?

In the introduction to this book I made the unsurprising contention that the purpose of training was to maintain or improve our sporting performance. But how do we achieve this?

When we train, we want to stimulate adaptations that increase our performance capability in our given sport. Every sport demands a particular set of performance capabilities, and so our training for sport needs to be focussed on developing one or more of these capabilities. In order to achieve this most training approaches are guided by the principle that the body will make adaptations that are specific to the demands that are imposed upon it (often called the SAID principle). Thus to improve a given performance capability we need to challenge it in training, the idea being that the resulting adaptation will increase our capability. In turn, the SAID principle suggests that our training will need to reflect the demands of the sport in order to ensure that adaptations are relevant to our sporting performance.

The previous paragraph is a very long-winded way of saying that training needs to be specific to the sport in question. The reason why I didn't simply just say this is that the idea of training specificity is one of the most widely known but least understood principles of training.

What is specific?

The SAID principle suggests that training for sports performance should be 'specific'. However, the meaning of specific is not defined. There is a risk that coaches interpret 'specific' in a very narrow sense, and consider that only training activities that closely mimic the sport will be appropriately specific. Instead, in many cases sport specific training can still be focussed on very general qualities that are then applied in a specific way in the sporting arena.

Coaches are often quite prepared to accept that energy system training can be general, while being very resistant to general approaches to the development of force expression capabilities. For instance, many coaches will be happy for their athletes to cross-train (swim, bike, run, etc) in order to develop their endurance capabilities, even if the sport itself doesn't involve swimming or biking or running. Similarly, many coaches believe that the specific endurance qualities needed in their sport will depend on the development of a strong aerobic base, and will thus be happy to spend time performing non-specific steady-state aerobic training activities like jogging. However, the same coaches will expect resistance training activities to closely replicate the movement patterns seen in the sport itself, and will find it hard to see how general athletic development activities translate to the field of play. We will explore the issue of what makes an activity 'specific' in the next chapter.

Transfer of training

The key to successful sports specific training is to ensure that any improvements in our capabilities 'transfer' to the sporting environment. That is, if we improve a particular capacity that this means that we are then able to perform better in our chosen sport. However, there are various mechanisms by which this transfer could occur. My friend Jon Goodwin and I, proposed the following categories for the transfer of training effects in a previous book:

- Primary transfer: the capability that has been increased is one that is directly used in the sport itself. For instance, if a volleyball player increases their vertical jumping ability as a result of training this might be expected to result in a primary transfer of training effects to sporting performance.

- Secondary transfer: there is an improvement in a general capability that underpins a more specific sporting ability. Good examples of this are improvements in general strength or aerobic capacity.

- Tertiary transfer: there is no direct mechanism for the transfer of performance effects, but the improvement in capability indirectly results in an improvement in performance. For instance, if an athlete becomes more robust as a result of their training then they may be able to practise and compete more frequently, and this will in turn improve their performance.

Clearly there will be some degree of overlap between these categories. Moreover, it is important to recognise that the categories are not listed in order of importance – for instance, many strength and conditioning coaches believe that their primary role is to keep their athletes healthy and available for practice and competition. These coaches are therefore most interested in the tertiary transfer of training effects to performance.

9 DYNAMIC CORRESPONDENCE

Improving our force expression capability

At the start of this book I suggested that our performance capabilities ultimately boil down to one of two things – our ability to access energy and our ability to express force. For this reason, a principal goal of training is to improve our ability to express force. However, we need to improve our ability to express force in the positions, postures and time constraints that are presented to us in our sport. We thus need to improve our 'sport specific' ability to express force. In order to do this the SAID principle tells us that we need to pick training activities that are specific to the force production demands of the sport. But how can we evaluate this?

As I alluded to in the previous chapter, for many coaches specific exercises are ones that mimic the sporting movement. These coaches only consider the kinematics* of the movement – they are interested only in whether the movements themselves are similar, and do not consider whether there are

---

* Kinematics is the term that is given to the study of movement without reference to the underlying forces. It is primarily the study of position, velocity and acceleration. Kinetics is the study of the forces themselves.

similarities in force production. Given that the force expression itself is the key variable, such an approach is unlikely to provide the basis for the best training decisions.

Dynamic correspondence

Dynamic correspondence is the term given to a more rounded method for evaluating the mechanical similarity of an exercise to a sporting skill. It is a method that was first popularised in the West by Siff and Verkhoshansky in their book *Supertraining*. In the method described by Siff, the dynamic correspondence of an exercise is established by comparing how closely it resembles the skill on five criteria:

- The amplitude and direction of movement: this is the kinematic criterion – do the joint movements in the exercise resemble those in the sporting skill?

- The region of accentuated force production: how do the joint angles when peak force is expressed compare?

- The dynamics of the effort: this is the criterion that encapsulates the need for overload – is the effort exerted in the exercise greater than that required in the sporting skill?

- The rate and time available for force production: how much time is available for force production in the sport? Does the exercise replicate this demand? Is the rate of force production greater in the training exercise?

- The regime of muscular work: how is force produced by the muscle in the sporting skill? Is force produced in the same way in the training exercise?

What is important to realise when evaluating dynamic correspondence is that a good training exercise does not need to correspond on every criterion. Rather, an exercise need only correspond on key criteria. In order to understand this, we need to introduce a couple more training principles – those of progressive overload and variation.

Progressive overload and variation

Training is generally described using the stress-adaptation model proposed by Hans Selye. According to this model, if we apply a stress to the body, the body's performance capability is first decreased (the so-called alarm phase), before adaptation occurs increasing the performance capability above its original value. In training, the stress that we apply to the body is our training bout. In order for training to be stressful, we need to 'overload' the body in some way – by challenging the body to do more than it is accustomed to. Over time, as we adapt and improve our performance capability, a given training session will no longer be challenging. For this reason we need to progressively increase the overload that we apply during training.

The need for variation in our training is related to the need for progressive overload. Again, if we simply perform the same training over and over again, we will experience diminishing returns – the training is not as stressful as it once was. By introducing variation to our training we can challenge our body in new ways, stimulating further adaptations.

How do these two concepts relate to dynamic correspondence? Fundamentally we are interested in improving our ability to express force in a way that is relevant to our sport. However, if we have practiced our sport for many years it may be difficult to overload aspects of the sports skill, and we will be very accustomed to performing them. In training therefore, we are seeking varied ways to challenge our force production capabilities in ways that will transfer to our sport. This is the beauty of using a method like dynamic correspondence. We can use the criteria to find exercises that allow us to overload particular aspects of sport specific force production. Again it is worth noting that we don't need to satisfy all criteria – in fact, by just focussing on particular aspects of force production we broaden the exercises available to us. This then allows us to provide progressive overload and variation to our training that far outstrips the possibilities offered by simply practising the sport itself.

Towards a refined model of dynamic correspondence

Dynamic correspondence is just one model for evaluating mechanical similarities, and it does have its weaknesses. For me, the most important of these is that the need for overload is not emphasised in the model, but is simply one of five criteria. It could be argued that for any exercise to dynamically correspond to a sporting skill it would need to satisfy the third criterion (the dynamics of the effort) – that is the effort exerted in the exercise is greater than the sporting skill. Similarly, the third criterion does not have an adequate focus on impulse production.

I would thus reframe the analysis of dynamic correspondence as follows. Firstly, the exercise must meet at least one of the two primary criteria:

- Possibility for overload: does the exercise provide the possibility of overload in terms of impulse production or factors that contribute to impulse production?* In particular (and as explicitly captured in Siff and Verkhoshanky's criteria) is the peak force or rate of force development higher in the exercise? Alternatively, does the exercise provide the opportunity for overload through repetition?

- Possibility for variation: does the exercise provide the possibility for variation. This might be considered to be particularly important when we consider the capability for force expression to be a skill. A discussion of this will be found in Chapter 10.

---

* The criterion of dynamics of the effort also permits overload in terms of other qualities such as velocity or power. Certainly this may be something that is relevant to consider, however in many cases the overload will ultimately be due to increased force or impulse production.

If the exercise satisfies one or both of the primary criteria, we can then evaluate its mechanical similarity to the sport by consideration of the secondary criteria:

- The movement kinematics;

- The direction of force/impulse production relative to the athlete;

- How is the limb coordinated to produce force?

- The time available to generate impulse;

- Body position and posture during peak force/impulse production;

- How does the muscle-tendon unit produce force?

The remainder of this book essentially comprises an exploration of these criteria. This will thus provide the vehicle for elucidating some of the more important biomechanical concepts that have implications for training.

10 DYNAMIC SYSTEMS THEORY

Guruism 101

In my first book, *The Little Black Book of Training Wisdom*, I cautioned coaches to be aware of the very human tendency to overcomplicate things. Motivations for this behaviour can be diverse. Sometimes we seek more complicated explanations in order to satisfy an internal desire to feel more expert. At the more nefarious end of the scale, skilful self-promoters understand the power of opaque, pseudoscientific systems in creating a guru persona, which can in turn lead to (relative) fame and wealth.

One of my personal bug bears has been the popularity of dynamic systems theory in explaining and guiding training. I believe that dynamic systems theory is attractive to coaches because it plays to our love of complexity, our need to feel expert and our desire to invent. However, the risk in giving primacy to dynamic systems considerations is that it can lead us to overlook other facets of the training process. This is not to suggest that the ideas professed by advocates of dynamic systems theory are incorrect, but rather that their importance is overstated.

What is dynamic systems theory?

Dynamic systems theory emerges from a consideration of classical mechanics and so it is 'biomechanics'. The theory is based upon the behaviour of differential equations. This definition is probably not that helpful for most readers, and leads to a string of further questions:

- "Well, what is a differential equation?"
    - "An equation that contains a derivative."
- "But what is a derivative?"
    - "The instantaneous rate of change of a variable."*
- "Pardon?"

---

* We have seen many examples of rate of change already in this book. For instance, acceleration is the rate of change of velocity.

$$a = \frac{\Delta v}{\Delta t}$$

When we calculate acceleration using the equation above, we calculate the change in velocity over a given period of time Δt. The instantaneous rate of change of velocity is the change if the time period Δt is infinitesimally small – i.e. it is as close to zero as it could be without actually being zero. We say that Δt tends to zero, and write this like this:

$$\Delta t \rightarrow 0$$

If we calculate the rate of change for these tiny, instantaneous time periods, then we indicate this by changing the 'Δ' to a 'd'.

$$a = \frac{dv}{dt} \quad \Rightarrow \quad a = \frac{\Delta v}{\Delta t}, \Delta t \rightarrow 0$$

The quantity $\frac{dv}{dt}$ is called the derivative of velocity with respect to time. It expresses the instantaneous acceleration at the precise time instant t.

And so on. In its essence, a good understanding of dynamic systems theory requires a working knowledge of calculus, the branch of mathematics that deals with rates of change. As most coaches don't have this background, it surprises me that dynamic systems theory is so popular. The good news is that, as we will see, it is not necessary to invoke dynamic systems theory in order to capture the ideas that its advocates are describing.

The basis for dynamic systems theory is that many systems can be usefully described (mathematically) by modelling the way in which they change. We have relied on a fantastic example of this already – Newton's 2nd Law relates the rate of change of velocity (acceleration) to the applied force. The fact that we have this calculation of rate of change within the equation, makes it a differential equation. We can make this more explicit if we write Newton's 2nd Law like this:

$$ F = ma \quad \Longrightarrow \quad \frac{\Delta v}{\Delta t} = \frac{F}{m} $$

Now let's say we wanted to use Newton's 2nd Law to calculate the final velocity of a body with a known mass when it is accelerated by a given force. In this case, it is useful to write Newton's 2nd Law in terms of the initial (v_1) and final (v_2) velocity:

$$ \frac{\Delta v}{\Delta t} = \frac{F}{m} \quad \Longrightarrow \quad \frac{v_2 - v_1}{\Delta t} = \frac{F}{m} $$

What we can see here is that in order to find the final velocity, we need to know the initial velocity. That is, to find the solution of this differential equation we need to know the 'initial conditions'.

Sometimes differential equations are highly sensitive to their initial conditions. What this means is that even small differences in the initial conditions can create very large differences in the solution. This is the basis of chaos theory – some systems are so sensitive to their initial conditions that it makes predicting their behaviour impossible. Even though we can create a mathematical model that describes the system (that consists of a system of differential equations) we can't find a useful solution because we can't specify the initial conditions with sufficient precision. The most famous example of this is probably 'the butterfly effect'. Climate models can exhibit chaotic behaviour, and the effects of this can be profound. For instance, a tiny change in the initial wind conditions caused by a butterfly flapping its wings in the United Kingdom, can result in a climate model predicting a tsunami in China.

At the other end of the spectrum is convergence. This is where a large range of initial conditions all lead to the same or similar solution. For instance, consider the crater depicted in Figure 7. If we drop a football anywhere within the crater, it will roll down the slope and end up in the bottom of the crater. We can have a large variation in the initial conditions (where we drop the football), but the outcome will be the same – the ball will come to rest at the bottom of the crater.

Figure 7. If we release a football at any point in this crater it will end up in a similar place at the bottom of the crater[1].

What is an attractor state?

In the training literature, there is a lot of talk about attractor states. An attractor state is simply a solution which exhibits convergence. That is, it is a solution that we will arrive at even if we start from a wide range of different initial conditions. So, for instance, we could describe the bottom of our crater as an attractor state.

The reason this is relevant to coaching and training is that we can use differential equations to describe movement – in particular, by using Newton's Laws. In this case, our initial conditions might be a range of variables that describe the task, environment or physical characteristics of the environment. Our attractor states would then be patterns of movement that emerge even when the constraints (task, environment, physiology) on the movement are quite varied. For instance, most people will exhibit a very similar gait pattern (i.e. walking) when they are asked to move from point A to point B at a relatively modest speed. This pattern is pretty stable even if the surface changes, or if the person is asked to carry a heavy weight, or if they are tall or short, etc etc. However, if we ask the person to increase their speed of movement the majority of people will transition to a different gait pattern (i.e. running) when their speed reaches around 4.5 miles per hour. Thus, the gait patterns of walking and running can be described as different attractor states that are relatively stable across a range of variables but that are sensitive to gait speed.

Self-organisation

In the example of gait, it is important to recognise that the transition from walking to running isn't 'ordered' by some central command unit like the brain. Instead, it is an emergent property of the system. What this means is that the system self-organises based on the interaction between its component parts. The ability of systems to self-organise results in some startling examples from nature (Figure 8).

Figure 8. Birds flocking are a good example of how natural systems can self-organise[2].

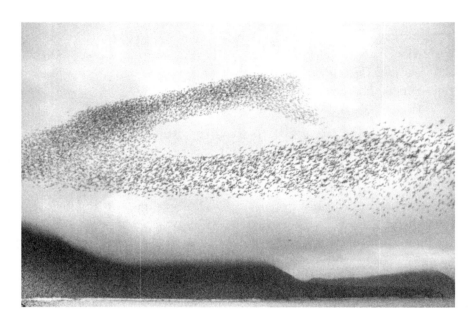

Variability

The final bit of theory that we need to talk about prior to really considering what dynamic systems theory might have to do with training is to consider variability within movement. Much of the thinking in this area is heavily influenced by Nicolai Bernstein's* studies of skilled performance in the middle of the 20th century. Bernstein studied the hammer strikes of blacksmiths (Figure 9). He found that although the outcome of the movement was very stable – that is the actual strike – the movement of the hammer could be very variable. Somewhat counter-intuitively, more skilled performers may exhibit more variability in certain aspects of their movements, and this may be beneficial to their performance.

---

* Interestingly, some accounts credit Bernstein with inventing the term biomechanics.

Figure 9. Variability in hammer trajectory of a skilled blacksmith[3].

What does all this have to do with training?

There is no doubt that there are aspects of the training and coaching process that can be well described by dynamics systems theory. The question is, is it helpful to describe training in these terms? Does dynamic systems theory provide us with insight or tools that would not be available to us if we didn't invoke it? I would suggest that the answer to these questions is no. I believe that we can capture much of the detail that is provided by dynamic systems theory if we understand self-organisation and variability.

Self-organisation and constraints-based learning

When it comes to learning a new skill, I guess that most often people will think that a coach will teach a skill in a very prescriptive way – showing the athlete the desired technique and then guiding them towards it through well-chosen cues. However, as we have just seen, when we move, our bodies and the environment form a self-organising system. This might suggest the possibility of a quite different process of skill acquisition – that is, given the right environment and conditions that a person can 'self-organise' in order to develop an appropriate technique themselves. In this paradigm, the role of the coach is then to create the appropriate conditions for effective skill development.

Constraints-based approaches to skill acquisition are founded on the latter view of the skill learning process. That is, the athlete is encouraged to explore a given movement to find their own most optimal technique. The problem with this is that self-organisation is difficult if the task is complex – for instance, an athlete who has never touched a tennis racket is unlikely to discover top spin – at least not for a long time. The role of the coach is therefore to provide constraints that facilitate the learning process, by providing movement problems that are appropriate to the skill level of the athlete, that allow them to experiment with movement, and that tend to encourage ways of movement that are technically optimal.

When we talk about 'constraints' it might lead some people to imagine that we are tying up one of the athlete's limbs (or similar). Of course, this is not the case, and effective constraints can often be quite modest. For instance, simply cueing an athlete to start from a particular start position is a constraint, and sometimes making sure an athlete starts from the right position is enough to encourage them to select the desired movement strategy. Similarly, verbal cues can also be constraints if they compel the athlete to try and move in a particular way.

It is important to recognise here that constraints-based approaches to coaching are not new and have been a part of the toolkit of many excellent coaches. Similarly, it is not necessary to invoke dynamic systems theory in order to understand how constraints-based approaches might work. It is enough to recognise that athletes can learn a great deal if they are allowed to explore movements themselves, and that a component of good coaching can be creating tasks or games that challenge athletes to move in new ways that are relevant to their sport.

What about dynamic correspondence?

A focus on dynamic systems theory has led to a resurgence of some weird and wonderful training exercises. However, whereas before such exercises were justified in the name of specificity, now the language of attractor states, constraints and variability is used in their support. But are these exercises any good?

In *The Little Black Book of Training Wisdom* I suggested that training can be characterised as improving both skills and capacities. Similarly, I proposed that some training can be viewed as involving the application of training stress in order to promote adaptation, whereas other types of training can be best described as practice. I think this distinction is helpful when considering the role of exercises derived from dynamic systems theory in training. I think such exercises should often be considered to be practice and are employed to improve skills. More explicitly, by adding variability into the skill execution, the athlete is able to explore the movement and find new strategies. It should be recognised that the ability to express force is a skill and that these exercises can be considered to meet the primary criteria of dynamic correspondence as they provide the possibility of variation. However, at the same time, the price of increasing variability is often in reducing the opportunity for the athlete to display high levels of force, and thus the possibility of overload is compromised.

My personal bias would be to ensure that some of our exercises provide the opportunity for overload such that we increase our force expression capacity. I thus tend to focus more on overload than I do on variation.

11 HORIZONTAL FORCE

Resolving vectors

Forces are vectors. When we describe a force we say how hard something is pushing or pulling (its magnitude) and in what direction. In order to understand forces we thus need to know a little bit more about vectors – in particular, how to add them. It's easiest to understand vector addition by visualising it geometrically. As seen in Figure 10a, the sum of a series of vectors can be represented by a single vector that runs from the start of the first vector to the end of the final vector.

This property of vectors is very handy when we are thinking about forces. In particular, what it means is that we can split any force into its horizontal and vertical components (Figure 10b; the sum of the two will add up to the original force). As we will see, this trick can considerably simplify the task of biomechanical analysis.

Figure 10. Understanding vectors: a) vector addition; b) resolution of a force into its horizontal and vertical components.

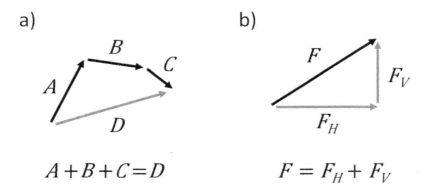

a)

$$A + B + C = D$$

b)

$$F = F_H + F_V$$

Ground reaction forces

We know from Newton's 2nd Law that if we want to accelerate in a given direction then we need a force to push us in that direction. We achieve this by generating a ground reaction force in the direction we want to move. This is achieved by pushing on the ground in the opposite direction to the one which we want to go. As a consequence of Newton's 3rd Law the ground then pushes back on us in the opposite direction – that is in the direction that we want to go (Figure 11).

Horizontal and vertical forces

We have just seen that if we want to accelerate or change the direction in which we are moving then we need to generate ground reaction forces in the desired direction. This means that acceleration or change of direction necessarily requires substantial horizontal forces – as we can see in Figure 11. This fact explains the correlation between the generation of horizontal force and acceleration/change of direction performance.

Figure 11. Generation of the ground reaction force in sprint acceleration.

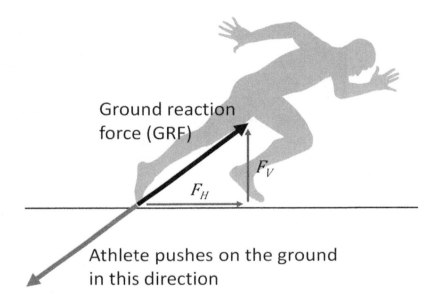

What coaches tend to neglect in their enthusiasm for horizontal forces, is that the athlete needs to exert substantial vertical forces as well. Firstly, they need to overcome the force of gravity. Secondly, in order to be able to take a step, they need to generate some flight time, and so need to propel themselves vertically.

Arguably, the requirements to overcome gravity and generate vertical propulsion are of primary importance and need to be satisfied before the athlete can even think about generating horizontal forces. However, it is probably more correct to observe that the production of horizontal and vertical forces are dependent upon one another – the athlete can only generate substantial horizontal forces if they also have the vertical lift to take a step. A focus on horizontal force alone is misguided.

One thing that is interesting to note here is that our athlete is not generating horizontal and vertical forces separately. Instead, they are exerting a force on the ground at an angle. We have resolved this force into its horizontal and vertical components as it is useful for our analysis – the horizontal component explains our horizontal acceleration whereas the vertical component counteracts gravity. However, this distinction is arbitrary. Rather than thinking about horizontal and vertical forces as separate qualities, it might be wise to think about the direction of the ground reaction force vector, and understand that this can be resolved into horizontal and vertical components if necessary for analysis. This in turn should help with the current over-emphasis on horizontal force production which is described in the next chapter.

12 FORCE-VECTOR THEORY

The worst name for a theory ever...

One of our revised criteria of dynamic correspondence was the direction of force production relative to the athlete. However, latterly some practitioners have contended that the specificity of an exercise should be evaluated based on the direction of the force relative to the Earth. They have named this idea the 'force-vector theory'. Apart from the fact that this is a terrible name (force is, by definition, a vector, so I am not sure what the theory is) it is also based on some confused thinking around coordinate frames.

Coordinate frames

When we describe the position of an object we generally use three dimensional coordinates. The coordinate system that we are all most familiar with is the Cartesian coordinate system. In order to specify the position of an object using Cartesian coordinates we need to have an origin from which we measure the distance of an object, and then three axes that are at right angles to one another. What is important to realise here is that both the position of the origin and the orientation of the axes is entirely arbitrary. As the position of the object is given relative to the coordinate system, provided we know the details of the coordinate system we can specify the position of the object precisely. The question then is what coordinate system should we use?

One thing that makes the choice of coordinate systems difficult is that everything around us is moving, as are we. In order to define our axes we need to 'fix' them to a particular object – the coordinate system then moves with that object. A sensible choice might be to fix our coordinate system relative to the Earth – we call this the 'world-fixed' or global coordinate system. Gravity provides us with a handy way to do this – the direction of vertical can be defined as being in the same direction as the force of attraction and then the remaining horizontal axes can be chosen to be perpendicular to the vertical axis (Figure 12). This is an acceptable solution, as in sport the movements that we are interested in take place relatively close to each other and so we can treat the surface of the Earth as being flat in our area of interest.

Sometimes it is helpful to specify positions relative to the athlete themselves. In this case we define a body-fixed or local coordinate system (Figure 12). In biomechanics we use a particular terminology to describe the position of things relative to the body-fixed coordinate system as shown in Figure 12. For instance, the axis that runs from the feet to the head is called the superior/inferior axis, and we would say that something that is closer to the head is more superior.

As can be seen in Figure 12, the orientation of the body-fixed coordinate system can change relative to the world-fixed frame. For instance, in the image on the left, with the athlete stood in the 'anatomical position', the two coordinate systems are aligned with one another. However, in the image of the athlete sprinting on the right, the orientation of the body-fixed coordinate system is very different to the world-fixed coordinate system. One important reason for the differing names that are given to the axes in the world- and body-fixed coordinate systems is to avoid confusion. The potential for this is apparent given that the two coordinate frames can be aligned with one another making it easy to mistake one for the other.

Figure 12. World-fixed (global) and body-fixed (local) coordinate systems (CS).

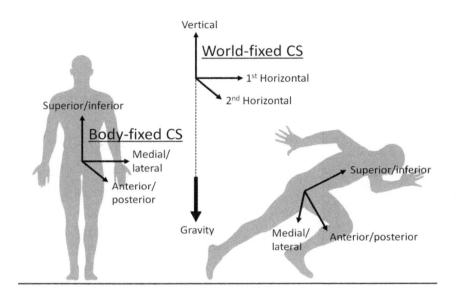

How do we direct force horizontally?

Our primary strategy for directing forces horizontally is to alter our body's orientation relative to the global frame – we lean forward (Figure 13). What is important to recognise here is that the direction of the force relative to the athlete is still largely unchanged. The athlete still extends their leg inferiorly generating a superiorly orientated ground reaction force, the force is just directed more horizontally relative to the global frame because the leg is now at an angle. This can be seen in the right hand image of Figure 13. If we rotate the athlete so that their body-fixed coordinate system is aligned to the world-fixed coordinate system we can see that the ground reaction force is predominantly vertical (superior relative to the athlete).

Figure 13. Force expression during sprint acceleration is horizontally inclined relative to the world-fixed coordinate system but largely superior (vertical) relative to the athlete.

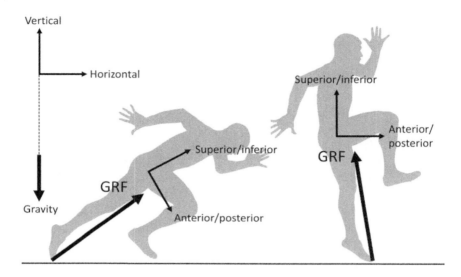

So, we have seen that during sprint acceleration, we predominantly create forces along the superior/inferior axis of the athlete. We could thus argue that any exercise where the direction of force expression is superior/inferior relative to the athlete would dynamically correspond on this criterion. For instance, exercises like squatting, deadlifting and Olympic style weightlifting all result in ground reaction forces that are superiorly directed and so would dynamically correspond to acceleration.

Where coaches sometimes get confused is because the direction of forces relative to the global frame are different. For instance, in acceleration there is a substantial horizontal component to the ground reaction force, whereas in squatting the force is largely vertical. This then leads these coaches to contend that the force production in these exercises is materially different. However, the direction of force production relative to the athlete is very similar.

Of course, the force production challenge that is presented to the two athletes in Figure 13 is not identical. In particular, the direction of gravity relative to the two athletes is different. This will mean that the direction of the ground reaction force vector relative to the two athletes will be different too and there will be differences in their movement strategies. However, the magnitude of this difference will be nowhere near as great as is suggested by proponents of the force-vector theory and the fundamental movement strategy is still to produce force on the superior-inferior axis by extending the leg forcefully.

Finally, there is mixed terminology...

Sometimes proponents of the force-vector theory are inconsistent in their use of terminology. For instance, it is common to see the argument that the hip thrust exercise is more specific to acceleration because force is directed horizontally in both activities (Figure 14). Let's unpack this claim.

Figure 14. Comparison of force expression relative to global and local coordinate frames in hip thrusting and sprint acceleration.

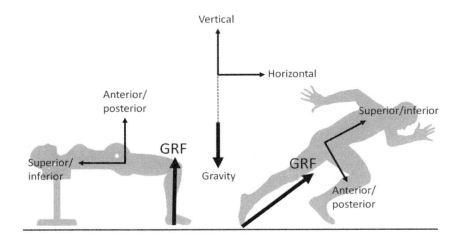

In acceleration, as we have seen, there is substantial horizontal force production relative to the global frame, but the direction of force

73

production relative to the athlete is inferior (i.e. vertical in the athlete's local coordinate frame). So the claim that acceleration is about horizontal force is clearly based upon a consideration of the global frame. In contrast, during hip thrusting the ground reaction forces are vertical relative to the global frame, but are directed anteriorly relative to the athlete (i.e. horizontally in the athlete's coordinate frame). The claim that hip thrusting is horizontal is thus based upon a consideration of the athlete fixed frame! The claim for correspondence is made by switching the coordinate frame in question for the two activities in order to fit the narrative.

13 PUSH, PULL, BOUNCE OR BLOCK

Creating vertical ground reaction forces

We have already seen that our main strategy for directing ground reaction forces is simply to reorient our body or our lower limb. But how do we generate ground reaction forces using our lower limb in the first place? In the majority of normal movements I would say there are essentially just four fundamental strategies which we employ to exert force on the ground with our lower limb: push, pull, bounce or block. The former two strategies are often referred to as squat and hinge within the strength and conditioning community and are widely known, whereas the latter two are less frequently acknowledged.

An understanding of the strategy that is used to create ground reaction forces is important in making training decisions. As we will see, these strategies differ markedly in terms of both the structures of the body that are used to exert force, and the specific mechanisms employed. For this reason, the strategy used in a sporting environment is a key consideration when thinking about the specificity of a given exercise. This chapter thus serves as an introduction to some of the later material in the book where I describe the production of force in more detail.

Push and pull

During push and pull strategies force is principally produced actively by the contractile tissue in muscle. If these terms are unfamiliar, don't worry, we will look at this in much more detail later. Essentially, what we see in these strategies is that a mechanical process takes place within the muscle itself, whereby energy is used to create force. During push and pull strategies muscle will undergo a change in length, which means there will be a substantial joint excursion.

A push or squat strategy (Figure 15) is where the knee and hip joints are extended or flexed in a synchronous pattern in order to express force. A push strategy is also seen in activities like vertical jumping – in this case there is a coordinated extension of the ankle, knee and hip (which is sometimes referred to as triple extension – see the next chapter).

Figure 15. Squat (left) and pull/hinge (right) patterns as exhibited in an air squat and a Romanian deadlift.

In contrast, in a pull or hip hinge, knee excursion is relatively minimal, and force is principally expressed by the extension or flexion of the hip joint. For instance, an example of hip hinging is the Romanian deadlift which is depicted in Figure 15. The identification of squat and hinge patterns isn't restricted to only athletic performance. For instance, in the occupational health literature it is common to see squat and stoop lifting techniques contrasted with one another.

Clearly, the choice of movement strategy has a profound impact on the musculature that is used to express force. For this reason, activities that rely on hip hinging strategies are often referred to as hip dominant as the muscles of the hip (glutes and hamstrings) are the prime movers. Hip dominant movements are often contrasted with knee dominant movements. Essentially, there is a continuum of movement strategies ranging from a very upright squat pattern that will require more involvement of the knee, all the way through to a strict Romanian deadlift which will largely involve the hip.

Individuals can show considerable variation in the way that they execute the same movement skills. As we saw in Chapter 4, some athletes jump using a very pure squat strategy (push strategy), with their torso very upright. In contrast, other athletes jump with a much more hip dominant strategy, with a torso that is quite flexed relative to the ground (pull strategy). As the discussion in Chapter 4 illustrated, often the rules or demands of a sport will determine the most appropriate technique.

Bounce and block

Both the push and pull strategies involve the active generation of force by muscle – we are creating force, as it were, from scratch. However, we can also express force passively. In this mode, we allow ourselves to collide with an external object, most often the ground, and forces are expressed during the impact. There are a number of different ways in which we can manage this impact, in order to most optimally use the force expression potential of the collision.

We can exemplify these strategies by considering what happens when we land after stepping off a box. If we want to remain on the ground after landing, we will need to exert an impulse that is equal to our momentum at the point of contact with the ground. Our strategy to do this will lie on a continuum between two extremes. At one end of the continuum we try and land as 'softly' as possible allowing our hips and knees to flex considerably, and trying to minimise the peak force during landing by taking a longer time to land. This is actually a push strategy for expressing force however, and we will discuss it in much more detail in Chapter 26. At the other end of the spectrum we could not try to cushion our landing at all, instead landing with straight legs. This landing would take less time to complete, but the peak force that we experienced would be much higher. The continuum that is described by these two extremes is the 'stiffness' of the landing.

The two strategies described above are based on remaining on the floor after landing. Alternatively, we might want to jump again after hitting the floor. We can do this by landing softly and coming to rest, and then jumping by using a further push strategy. However, we could try to bounce off the floor instead – using the momentum of our collision to propel us back into the air.

The three strategies described here can be intuitively understood by consideration of Figure 16. Let's say we drop three objects of the same mass, a teddy bear, a rock and a basketball, from the same height. The teddy bear will land softly, because it will deform considerably on landing, reducing the peak forces. In contrast, the rock will land with a crash, and if it is brittle might even break, due to the larger force experienced on landing. Finally, the basketball will, of course, bounce.

Figure 16. Dropping a teddy bear, a rock and a basketball.

In terms of our force expression strategies, the basketball unsurprisingly represents the bounce strategy. In human movement, during a bounce strategy we try to organise our musculoskeletal system such that the collision with the ground stretches our elastic tissues. We can visualise this by thinking of our lower limb as a spring that is compressed as we collide with the ground, producing force. When the spring returns to its original length, more force is produced.

A block, or vault strategy is represented by the rock. This may seem like a strange way to express force given the risk associated with the high peak forces and the fact that we don't seem to be using the tissues of the leg at all. I think this is one reason why block strategies are often overlooked in analyses of human movement. However, there are situations where we do block to produce force. For instance, when throwing a javelin or bowling a cricket ball, athletes block on the last step. This allows them to convert their momentum into a very high ground reaction force.

Bounce and block strategies are seen during gait, and in fact, some popular simple models of gait make these strategies very explicit (Figure 17). For instance, many of the key characteristics of running can be captured using a 'spring-mass' model. Here, the leg is simply modelled as a spring, and the body as a point mass. As can be seen in Figure 17, during each foot contact, when the foot first makes contact with the ground the spring is compressed in order to halt the athlete's downward momentum. Later in the gait cycle, the spring expands and it is this force which launches the athlete into their next stride. Clearly, the spring-mass model provides a vivid illustration of the bounce strategy – under this model, we bounce from foot contact to foot contact.

Figure 17. The spring-mass model of running (left) and compass-gait model of walking (right).

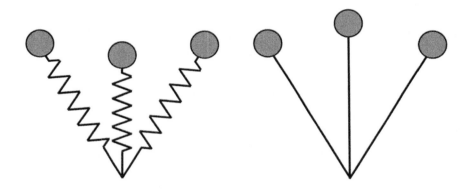

A similar model is also sometimes employed to describe walking. The only difference is that in this case the leg is modelled as a rigid beam. In contrast to the spring-mass model, where the mass of the athlete compresses the leg, during walking the athlete 'vaults' over their rigid leg.

Of course, there is a blend of strategies

Although I have described the push, pull, bounce and block strategies as being distinct, in practice there will be a blend of strategies during movement. For instance, during vertical jumping which I earlier suggested was principally a push strategy, there is also an element of 'bounce', particularly as the athlete transitions from moving down in the countermovement to moving upwards in the propulsive portion of the jump (this is often referred to as the stretch-shortening cycle). It is also of critical importance to recognise that athletes differ in terms of their reliance on different force production strategies. For instance, some athletes are more bouncy and tend to select movement strategies that allow them to use their momentum to create force. Alternatively, other athletes show a preference towards the active production of force through push and pull strategies.

The gross movement strategy used by an athlete to express force will have a profound effect on the way in which the structures of the musculoskeletal system are employed and loaded during movement. For this reason, the movement strategy used by an athlete will be an important consideration when choosing training modalities.

14 DISTRACTED BY TRIPLE EXTENSION

What is triple extension?

So, as we have just seen, many athletic movements involve us extending our leg to exert force into the ground. These movements generally require the coordinated extension of the ankle, knee and hip – hence triple extension. An example that is often given of a triple extension pattern is the 'clean pull' in Olympic weightlifting (Figure 18).

Triple extension certainly occurs in a range of movements, so why do I say people get distracted by it? In order to understand this we need to talk about observability bias.

Figure 18. Triple extension at the end of the second pull in Olympic-style weightlifting.

Observability bias

One of Steve Magness' 'Rules of Everything' is that "we overemphasise the importance of what we can measure and what we already know". In coaching this manifests itself in what I call 'observability bias'. That is, we can only coach what we can see, and this will lead us to focus on the aspects of the skill that are most visually evident to us. However, the problem here is that the most obvious things may not be the most important.

A good example of observability bias is triple extension. How do we assess whether an effective triple extension has occurred? In high speed extension movements it is often difficult for the inexperienced eye to pick up fine technical details during the course of the movement. Instead, the easiest position to spot is the fully extended end position (for instance, the end of the second pull that is depicted in Figure 18). Naturally, if a coach is particularly interested in improving an athlete's triple extension this can lead them to cue the athlete to ensure that they hit a fully extended end position. Unfortunately, this can often be counter-productive.

Full extension is follow through…

The fully extended end position seen in a range of triple extension movements (e.g. jumping and weightlifting) is actually a consequence of things that happen earlier in the movement. For instance, Figure 19 shows a series of stills of an athlete jumping side-by-side with the force-time graph from the movement. As the top image shows, the end of peak force expression occurs when the lower limb is still relatively flexed. From this point onwards, force production drops rapidly, such that in the fully extended position, force production is zero. Essentially, it is the momentum that the athlete accrued in the earlier part of the jump that carries them through to the fully extended position. The instant at which full extension occurs is of minor importance to the execution of the movement as little force is expressed at this time.

The problem with cueing an athlete to hit a fully extended position is that you are emphasising a less important position. This isn't always necessarily a bad thing – such a cue might be effective if the athlete complies with it by exerting more force at the appropriate time and then has a greater 'follow through'. However, there will be negative consequences if the cue results in the athlete delaying their peak effort until later in the movement.

A misguided focus on the end position is frequently a problem in Olympic weightlifting. This is because, after exerting the maximum possible impulse on the bar, the athlete then needs to reverse their body's direction of motion and descend to catch the bar. Over-cueing the athlete to hit an extended position can badly compromise an athlete's technique by making them slow to get under the bar. This then compounds the problem of the athlete reserving their effort until too late in the movement.

Figure 19. Force production during vertical jumping[4].

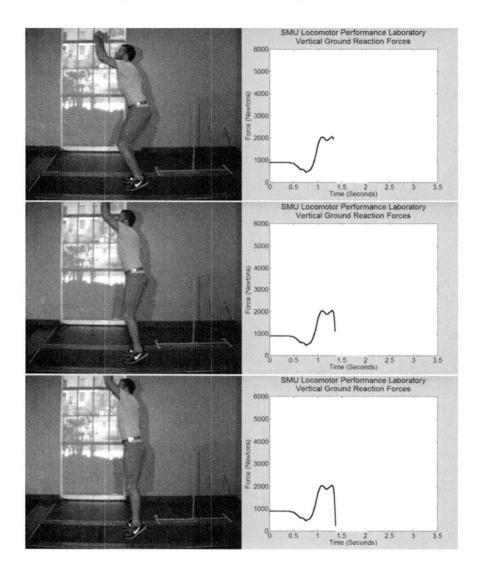

The triple extension myth

Clearly, running also involves a triple extension pattern of the lower limb (Figure 20). The latter part of the extension takes place when the foot is behind the athlete. What is important to realise is that for many elite sprinters the leg will not be fully extended at the point the foot leaves the ground. However, to the untrained eye it can appear like full extension is reached. The legs move quickly when we sprint, it is hard to pick out the shapes that athletes make, and it seems logical that full extension should occur.

Figure 20. Kinogram of an elite sprinter[5] (personal best 100m performance 9.94s) running at 11.1ms[-1].

Similar to jumping or weightlifting, coaching an athlete to focus on fully extending at push-off can have a disastrous effect. Again, force production should be miniscule at this point, and instead the athlete should be bringing the leg forward to prepare for its next contact with the ground. Asking an athlete to emphasis push-off will cause them to spend more time on the ground which will in turn make them slower.

15 MOMENTS

External and internal

So far, we have just considered the external mechanics of the athlete. In particular, we have talked a great deal about the external force that acts on the athlete's feet – the ground reaction force. In the last two chapters, we have begun to consider how the joints and segments of the body are coordinated to produce the ground reaction force. In this chapter we will start to look beneath the skin, to see how the internal forces that are produced by muscle are converted into external forces.

Linear to rotational

In order to understand the function of our musculoskeletal system we need to understand levers. An example of a lever within the musculoskeletal system is illustrated in Figure 21. A lever is a rigid body that rotates around a pivot point. In our bodies, our bones act as levers, that are pivoted by other bones at our joints. This means that the linear forces that are exerted by our muscles are converted into 'rotational forces' that act upon our bones. A 'rotational force' is called a moment or a torque.

Figure 21. Bones often act as levers within musculoskeletal systems[6].

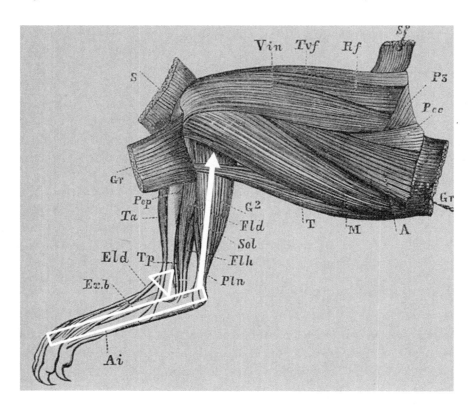

The magnitude of the moment (*M*) or turning force is dependent on two things (Figure 22). The first is, of course, the magnitude of the force (*F*) that is exerted by the muscle. The second is the perpendicular distance (*d*) from the muscle's line of action to the pivot (that is, the joint). The moment is simply the product of the force and the distance:

$$M = F \times d$$

Figure 22. The turning force or moment (M) acting to rotate a lever about a pivot is the product of force (F) and distance (d).

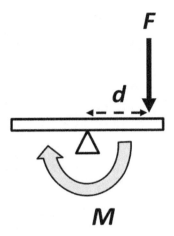

Figure 23. A large force (F) applied close to the pivot (d), results in a smaller force (f) further away from the pivot (D).

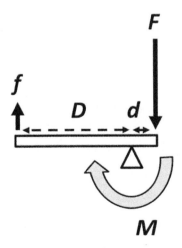

One characteristic of our musculoskeletal systems that has important ramifications is that the distance from our muscle insertions to our joints is normally much smaller than the distance from the joint to the place where we intend to apply force. You can visualise this by again looking at Figure 21 – the distance from the cat's joint to its paw is several times larger than from joint to muscle insertion. This means that the internal forces created by our muscles and the actual external forces that we are able to exert on our environment are typically governed by a relationship like that depicted in Figure 23. That is, the magnitude of the forces in our muscles is generally much greater than the external force that we are able to express.

Modest external forces equate to large internal forces

The peak ground reaction force seen during the take-off of a vertical jump is typically in the range of 2-3 times body weight. However, the internal forces are several times greater than this – for instance, the internal knee forces can be 7-9 times body weight in each knee. There are two principal reasons for this. Firstly, as we have seen, the muscles generally have a mechanical disadvantage due to the nature of most musculoskeletal levers. Secondly, the muscles tend to pull the articular surfaces of the joints together, increasing the internal forces (Figure 24).

If we appreciate the magnitude of the internal forces that athletes experience during movement it can really help in understanding injury. Thankfully, our musculoskeletal system is built to tolerate these large loadings. For instance, the anterior cruciate ligament (ACL) which is a frequently injured structure of the knee is able to bear a force of approximately 2000N before it fails. That is, if you attached one end of the ACL to the roof, you could hang a weight of up to around 200 kg from it and be fairly confident it wouldn't break!

Figure 24. The cat[6] is isometrically* pressing its paw against the ground creating a ground reaction force F_{GRF}. Because the limb is not moving, this force must be balanced by an equal and opposite force acting at the cat's joint ($-F_{GRF}$). The ground reaction force is a result of the muscle force F_M which also must be balanced by an equal and opposite force acting at the joint ($-F_M$). The internal joint contact force is thus $-(F_M + F_{GRF})$ which is much greater than the external ground reaction force F_{GRF}.

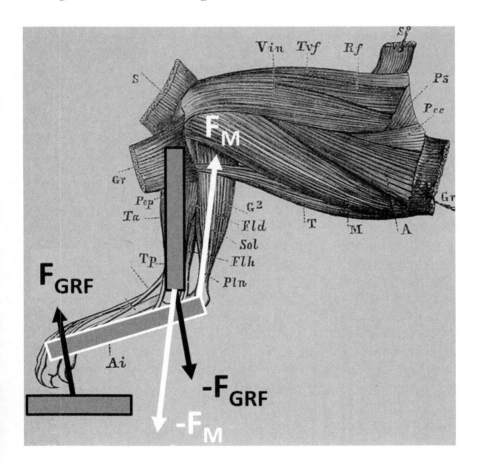

---

* We call a muscle action isometric if the muscle exerts force without changing length.

16 CREATING TORQUE?

Moment versus torque

In the previous chapter, we learnt how to calculate a moment. A moment is sometimes called a torque. In some places these words are used interchangeably and in others they have subtly different meanings. For our purpose, I will take them as describing the same thing – the turning force.

Supple leopards

Kelly Starrett, the author of *Becoming a Supple Leopard*, has popularised the idea of twisting a joint in order to 'create torque'. For instance, during squatting he contends that we should screw our feet into the floor to create hip torque. My purpose in this short chapter is not to discuss whether this is good advice, but rather simply to talk about the use of terminology here.

As we have just seen, a torque is created whenever a linear force creates a turning effect. Our bodies are machines that do just this – whenever a muscle expresses a force that acts to rotate a joint we have created a torque. Thus, when we squat, we create 3 dimensional torque at all of the involved joints. This occurs whether we screw our feet into the floor or not.

Of course, if we screw our feet into the floor, we might stimulate more activity in the muscles of the leg and hip. This in turn might increase the torque that is created at the hip. It is not therefore inherently wrong to say that screwing our feet into the floor creates torque. However, I believe that the appropriation of the term torque to describe a particular motor control strategy can lead to misunderstanding, and this has been reinforced by conversations that I have had with coaches and students. I worry that the use of a scientific-sounding term like torque can convince coaches and athletes that the movement strategy being advocated is correct. This then conceals the actual issues that are under debate and the claims that are being made. What is the effect of twisting a joint during performance of a movement? Does it result in a greater moment that facilitates the movement execution? Does it increase the moment in the direction of the twisting movement, and if it does, what structures are applying this force? Does this increase joint stability in a desirable way?

17 POSTURE

The moment arm

In Chapter 15, I defined the moment to be equal to the product of force and the perpendicular distance from the line of action of the muscle to the joint. However, I didn't really elaborate on the meaning of perpendicular distance. Essentially, we need to find a line that intersects the line of action of the muscle at a right angle, and that passes through the joint centre (Figure 25). This perpendicular distance is often described as the moment arm of a muscle.

The importance of the moment arm

The moment arms of our muscles can be highly dependent upon our body posture. This is because, even though the attachment points of our muscles are fixed relative to the joint centres, the lines of action of the muscles vary as we flex and extend our joints. This means that the moment arms of the muscles can vary considerably, and in particular, are dependent on joint angles (Figure 26).

Figure 25. The turning force or moment acting to rotate a lever about a pivot is the product of force (*F*) and the perpendicular distance between the line of action of the force and the pivot (*d*).

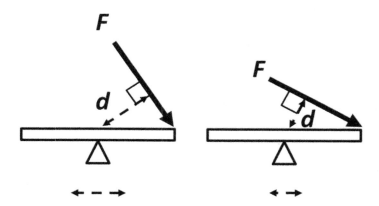

Figure 26. Flexion or extension of a joint can cause profound differences in the magnitude of the moment arm.

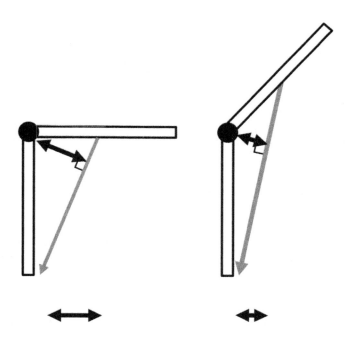

Our ability to exert force is therefore highly dependent upon our body posture. That is, the force we can exert, and even the muscles we use to achieve a given task are dependent upon our joint angles during the task. This then provides a strong rationale for considering the correspondence of joint angles when evaluating the specificity of a training exercise and a sporting skill. In particular, we want to improve our ability to express force in body postures, and with joint angles, that are seen in the competitive environment.

Strength gains are specific to joint angle

One question that we have not addressed is whether the results of strength training are affected by joint angles. If we train at a particular joint angle, will our strength gains be realised across the full range of joint excursion or be local to the joint angle at which train? Unfortunately, there is some pretty good evidence that at least some types of strength training are joint angle specific. For this reason, a consideration of body posture and joint angles is important when choosing training activities.

18 HOW DOES MUSCLE WORK?

The functional anatomy of muscle

In order to understand how muscle works we need to take a look at its structure. We can then use biomechanical reasoning to gain insight into the function of muscle, and then in turn, extrapolate the meaning of this for training.

Whole muscle is composed of bunches of muscle fibres. Each muscle fibre itself, is comprised of a bunch of myofibrils (Figure 27A). A myofibril consists of a series of sarcomeres joined together end to end. The sarcomere is the functional contractile element of muscle – that is, actions within the sacromere are responsible for the active production of force by muscle.

The key functional components of the sacromere are the proteins actin and myosin. These are arranged in filaments that lie parallel to one another (Figure 27B). When a muscle contracts (shortens) the actin filaments slide over the myosin filaments, which allows the sarcomere to shorten (Figure 28). Even though the length change of a sarcomere is objectively small, because there are many sarcomeres in series within a myofibril, the myofibril itself can undergo substantial length changes.

Figure 27. Anatomy of a muscle fibre (A) and a sarcomere (B)[7].

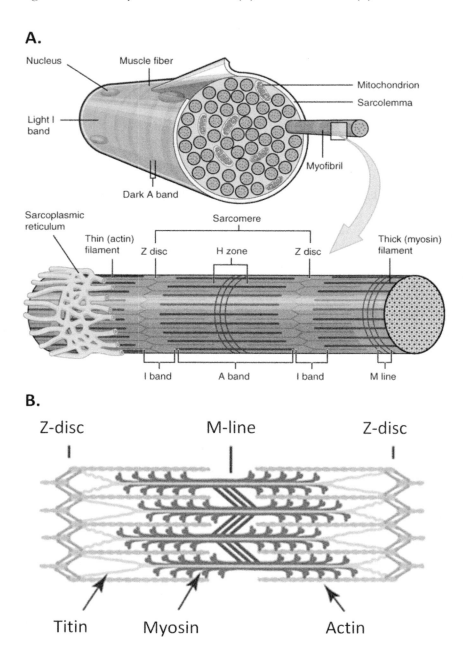

Figure 28. Sliding filament theory[8].

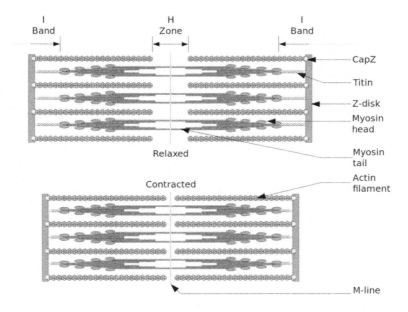

Sliding filament theory

Sliding filament theory is the name given to the mechanism of muscle length change (for obvious reasons). However, what causes this movement? If you study Figure 27B, you will see that the myosin filament has lots of branches shooting off it. These are called 'myosin heads' although a better name might be myosin hands or grabbers. These myosin heads create the movement of the filaments in a process called cross-bridge cycling.

Figure 29. Cross-bridge cycling and the power stroke[9].

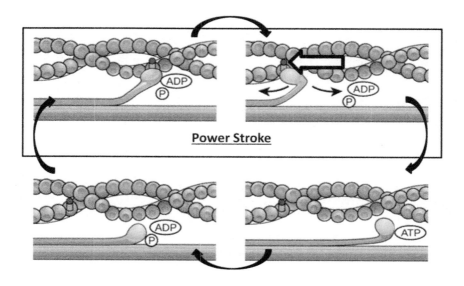

Figure 29 depicts the process of cross-bridge cycling. Firstly, the myosin head attaches to an 'active site' on the actin filament. The head then bends backwards in the power stroke, pulling the actin filament with it. The myosin head is then released from the actin filament, before reconnecting to the next active site along the actin molecule.

What is important to notice in Figure 29 are the molecules of ADP (adenosine diphosphate) and ATP (adenosine triphosphate). The energy that we get from the food we eat is chemically stored within the ATP, and as the ATP is converted to ADP it provides the energy that powers the process of cross-bridge cycling. This is thus the mechanism by which chemical energy is converted into mechanical work.

An appreciation of the mechanics of muscle contraction (that is sliding filament theory) is important to understand the behaviour of whole muscle. In particular, the amount of force that can be expressed by the muscle is affected by three things:

- The number of cross-bridges that are formed – more cross-bridges means a greater force;

- The time available for cross-bridges to form and exert force – more time means more force;

- The type of contraction – that is, is the muscle staying the same length, shortening or lengthening?

We will take a look at these factors in the next chapter.

19 THE BEHAVIOUR OF MUSCLE

Muscle contraction properties

The force that can be expressed by a muscle is dependent upon a number of factors including the length of the muscle, the velocity of contraction, the time available to produce force, and the contraction regime. Many of these properties can be understood by reference to sliding filament theory.

The force-length relationship of muscle

The force that a muscle can express is dependent upon its length. The explanation for this lies in remembering that force is created within active tissue by the process of cross-bridge cycling. In particular, if more cross-bridges are able to be formed then more force can be expressed. The length of the muscle is an important determinant of how many cross-bridges can be formed.

It is easiest to understand the argument if we just consider what is going on in one sarcomere. As can be seen in Figure 30, when the sarcomere is at optimal length, the actin fibres overlap all of the myosin heads, which means that they are all available to form cross-bridges and generate force. As the sarcomere lengthens, the actin fibres are displaced relative to the myosin, meaning that some of the myosin heads are not overlapped by actin. This means that not all of myosin heads are available to form cross-bridges. Ultimately, at long sarcomere lengths there may be no overlap of actin and myosin fibres meaning that no cross-bridges can be formed. Conversely, when the sarcomere is shortened below its optimal length, the actin fibres on either side of the M-line begin to overlap each other. This also inhibits some myosin heads from forming cross-bridges. In addition, when the myosin filament reaches the Z-disc at the end of the sarcomere, no further shortening is possible (Figure 30).

Figure 30. Sarcomere length-tension relationship[10].

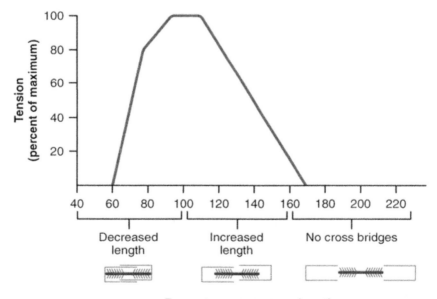

The mechanics of cross-bridge cycling mean that muscle exhibits a force-length relationship, and that each muscle has an optimal force-generating length. Clearly, the length of a muscle is determined by an athlete's posture as flexing a joint will change the length of a muscle that spans it. This provides another reason why we are stronger in some positions than others, in addition to the variation in moment arms seen in Chapter 17.

The force-velocity relationship of muscle

The mechanics of cross-bridge cycling also mean that muscles exhibit a kind of force-velocity relationship. In particular, it takes time for cross-bridges to form and to express force*. What this means is that, if more time is available, then more cross-bridges will form, and that the potential for force production is higher. The most important factor that determines the time available for cross-bridge formation is the contraction (or extension) speed of the muscle fibre. If the muscle is shortening quickly, then the actin and myosin filaments are sliding past one another more quickly – and thus cross-bridge formation is hampered. Figure 31 describes the force-velocity relationship of muscle. The right hand side of the graph represents the shortening of muscle. What we can see is that there is a characteristic hyperbolic relationship between force and velocity.

Figure 31. Force-velocity relationship of muscle[11].

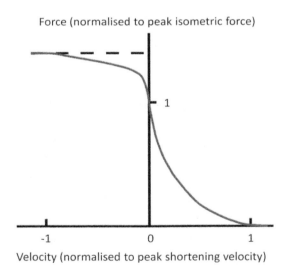

Force (normalised to peak isometric force)

-1   0   1

Velocity (normalised to peak shortening velocity)

---

* This can also be explained in terms of physiological mechanisms, but is a level of detail that I don't want to explore in this book.

Contraction regime

We can also learn some other important characteristics of muscle behaviour from Figure 31. In particular, we can see that maximal force production is also dependent on the type of contraction. Force production capacity is highest during eccentric contractions (i.e. when the muscle is lengthening), next highest during isometric muscle action (i.e. when the muscle is not changing length), and is lowest during concentric muscle actions (i.e. when the muscle is shortening). There have been attempts to explain this behaviour in terms of the mechanics of the cross-bridges too, but these explanations are more controversial, and the mechanisms are less well understood.

What we have seen is that the contraction regime has a big influence on both the way that force is produced and the overall potential for force expression. The one big take away from the material presented in this and the previous chapter is therefore that contraction regime is important when considering the specificity of training.

A force-velocity relationship?

So have we found a force-velocity relationship? Well, probably not. How can we resolve this apparent contradiction? What is important to realise is that when we describe muscular contraction dynamics we are describing how force is constrained relative to contraction velocity in muscle (and vice versa). For instance, the contraction velocity sets a limit on the maximum force capability of the muscle. If we were to state this more precisely, we have found a relationship between the maximum force and the maximum contraction velocity. This is different to arguing that force is the cause of velocity, which is the mistaken Aristotelian view of mechanics that was described in the first chapter. Finally, it is also important to note that the relationship we have found here is a property of muscle, not a universal law. In the real world, generally, there is not a relationship between force and velocity.

20 THE FORCE-VELOCITY RELATIONSHIP!

What about human movement?

So we have established that in isolated muscle there is a relationship between maximum force and contraction velocity. It is common for coaches to assume that the existence of this relationship at the muscle level automatically means that the same relationship will apply to human movement itself. However, human movement is complex, and the contraction dynamics of muscle are just one set of factors. As we have already seen, the linear forces that are expressed by muscles are converted into rotational torques. As we will see in a couple of chapters time, muscle is not the only producer of force during movement, and the other components of the 'muscle-tendon unit' play a role in the expression of force. In addition, human movement is the product of the synchronised activation of many muscles, and there is no guarantee that the behaviour of one muscle fibre in isolation is the same as the coordinated behaviour of many.

The force-velocity continuum

Despite the fact a force-velocity relationship in human movement is not a necessary consequence of the pseudo force-velocity relationship seen in muscle, it is common for training texts to present a force-velocity continuum of exercises that can be used to inform training decisions (Figure 32). Unfortunately, such a classification of exercises does not really bear even the most cursory critical examination.

Figure 32. A typical force-velocity continuum of exercises.

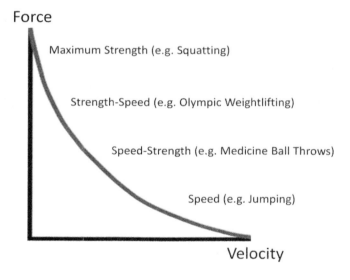

Let's take a critical look at the force-velocity curve by considering a typical maximum strength exercise like squatting, and comparing it to a strength-speed exercise like Olympic weightlifting. The force-velocity curve suggests that during squatting, an athlete will exhibit higher forces but move at a lower velocity, than during an Olympic lift. But is this true? Certainly, the speed of movement during Olympic weightlifting will be higher than squatting. However, the forces expressed during weightlifting are also likely to be higher as well! It is thus probably incorrect to classify squatting as being a higher force exercise than Olympic weightlifting.

Another example of this is given in Figure 33. In this case, the data presented here is taken from a cohort of athletes who performed both a squat (maximum strength exercise) and a jump squat (strength-speed exercise). Again, we can see here that the performance of the strength-speed exercise resulted in higher velocities of execution and peak forces than the strength exercise at each of the loads utilised (and in this case the two activities are markedly similar).

Figure 33. Peak force and velocity during squatting and jump squatting[12].

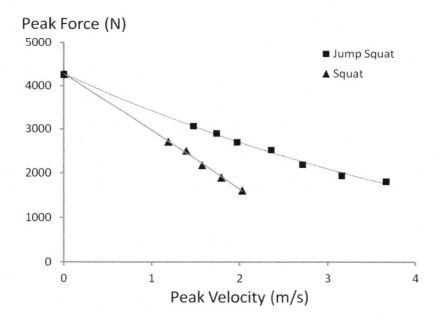

Similar arguments can be advanced when considering other parts of the force-velocity curve. For instance, is sprinting really a low force activity? – it involves the expression of pretty high forces through just one leg, and if you double those forces to compare to squatting...

The load-velocity continuum

I think that what coaches are trying to express when they talk about a force-velocity continuum is actually a load-velocity relationship. That is, if we are performing a movement with more load, that we will move more slowly. If the y-axis in Figure 32 was relabelled as load, then the relationship described in Figure 32 would probably be correct. Similarly, such a classification of exercises would then be potentially useful for exercise classification and programming.

But if this is the case, does it matter? Doesn't this amount to the same thing? I would argue, emphatically, no. When we refer to a force-velocity continuum like this we are conflating force with load. This quickly leads to misunderstanding. We don't necessarily require a large load to express high forces, and in sport we are often most interested in increasing the force that an athlete can apply against a fixed load – their own body weight.

But is there a force-velocity relationship for movement?

So I have argued that the presence of a force-velocity relationship in muscle doesn't necessarily mean there is a force-velocity relationship in human movement. However, at the same time, it does not preclude it. So is there one?[*]

We have already seen that this question is pretty difficult to answer if we are comparing different movements. However, can we at least answer the question by studying one particular exercise, and comparing the force and velocity characteristics when using different loads?

Such an analysis is presented in Figure 33 for two different movements, the squat and squat jump. Certainly at first glance, each of the movements seems to exhibit a linear relationship between force and velocity. However, we need to be careful that we are not falling into our old trap of conflating

---

[*] I am so sorry if it feels like we are going round and round in circles.

an instantaneous relationship between force and velocity with the impulse-momentum relationship.

The important thing to notice in Figure 33 is that it presents peak force and velocity during the movements. Peak force and peak velocity may not occur at the same time. For instance, Figure 34 shows that during vertical jumping, peak force and velocity occur at very different times. Figure 33 is thus probably not reflective of an instantaneous relationship – it does not present the force that is seen at a particular velocity. Instead, we have a comparison of how the peak forces and velocities during the whole movement vary based on different loads.

Figure 34. Relationship between peak force and peak velocity during vertical jumping.

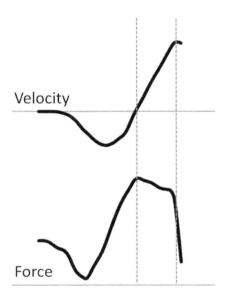

We can go further in this analysis. For a movement like squatting or jumping where we start from rest our peak velocity is the same as our change in velocity up to that point. In addition, our change in velocity is determined by the amount of net impulse we impress up until that point (as a consequence of the impulse-momentum relationship). So what we are actually plotting in Figure 33 is the relationship between peak force and net impulse over the propulsive period. What we are showing here is the approximately linear relationship between the peak force and total net impulse in these movements.

We could express this in a different way. If we were to assume that the peak force is linearly related to the total impulse*, then the y-axis in Figure 33 can be considered to be a proxy for net impulse. Similarly, the x-axis is a proxy for change in velocity (i.e. change in momentum). In this instance, we have thus shown that there is an approximately linear relationship between net impulse and change in momentum. That is, given these assumptions (and it should be noted that they are huge assumptions), we have experimentally proven the impulse-momentum relationship.

The jury is out

The point of this analysis is to show, at length, that the presentation of data showing a linear relationship between the peak force and peak velocities seen in a complete movement, where each data point is a repetition of the movement performed with a different load, is, categorically, not evidence of an instantaneous force-velocity relationship. Instead, it simply represents how the relationship between peak force and net impulse varies across different loads. This is not to say that this information is not interesting (it is). However, if we want to establish if there is a force-velocity relationship during movement we need to compare instantaneous forces and velocities during movement.

This point is particularly important as there has been a trend in the literature to present results like those seen in Figure 33, and to claim that these are evidence of a force-velocity relationship. They are not, and this is simply another example of the type of confusion between force-velocity,

---

* In other words, that the shape of the force-time graphs for each load is approximately the same.

force-acceleration and impulse-momentum relationships that was described earlier in this book.

This is not to say that there might not be a force-velocity relationship for certain exercises within human movement. However, I think it is most fair to say that the jury is out on this issue at present.

21 CONSTANT FORCE AND ACCELERATION

Or, your biomechanics textbook is not quite right...

So far in this book I haven't actually given the formulae to calculate impulse or work. In many biomechanics textbooks the formulae that are given are:

$$I = Ft \qquad \text{and} \qquad W = Fx$$

However, in mathematics textbooks you will see the following:

$$I = \int F \, dt \qquad \text{and} \qquad W = \int F \, dx$$

So which is right? In actual fact, they both are – but with one caveat. The formulae that are given first here only apply when force is constant – i.e. the level of force applied is unchanging. The formulae that include the squiggly 'integration' sign are more general – they apply whether the force is constant or variable. This distinction will be important to understand the material in the next chapter.

The reason for the simplified presentation of these formulae is clear – most sports science students have not studied calculus and will not have seen the integration sign before. What is more important is to consider whether the omission of this detail from biomechanics textbooks matters? I would say yes, and no! On the one hand, I think the simplified representation makes it easier for coaches and students to acquire some intuitive understanding of what impulse or work are. However, at the same time, it is really important to appreciate that when we apply forces in the sporting environment, the application of force is rarely constant. Have a look at the force-time graphs in Figure 1 – the application of ground reaction forces over time is highly non-linear. In these cases it is almost impossible to apply the simplified equations – what force value would we use?

Equations of constant acceleration

One topic that is typically covered very early on in biomechanics textbooks is the equations of constant acceleration. These are relationships between kinematic variables (displacement, velocity and acceleration) that only apply when acceleration, and therefore force*, is constant. For completeness, I present these equations below, where d is displacement, u is initial velocity, v is final velocity, a is acceleration and t is time.

$$v = u + at$$

$$d = ut + \frac{1}{2}at^2$$

$$v^2 = u^2 + 2ad$$

$$d = \frac{1}{2}(u + v)t$$

---

* Assuming the mass of the moving object is also constant. This is normally the case, but there are some situations where it is not. For instance, when a rocket takes off it burns fuel at such a rate that the mass of the rocket changes appreciably as it accelerates during take-off.

$$d = vt - \frac{1}{2}at^2$$

The classic example that is normally presented along with these equations is the calculation of the flight of a projectile, for instance a javelin, a basketball or a bullet. Once a projectile has been 'projected' by the application of some external forces and it is flying through the air, the only force acting upon it is a result of gravity (we ignore air resistance). As gravity is a constant, the projectile experiences a constant acceleration of $9.81ms^{-2}$ towards the centre of the Earth.

When we jump, after we leave the floor we can also be considered to be a projectile. This then provides the context in which coaches will likely be most familiar with the equations of constant acceleration. A common method for calculating vertical jump height is through the use of a timing mat, which provides us with the time of flight of an athlete during their jump. What we want to find is the peak displacement (height) during the jump. If we divide the time of flight in half, it gives us the time it takes an athlete to reach the peak height of their jump. Similarly, at the peak of their jump, the athlete's velocity will be zero — they are momentarily at rest until their velocity begins increasing as they fall to the floor. We also know that the athlete is experiencing a constant acceleration of $-9.81ms^{-2}$ (gravity). We thus know a, v and t, and we are trying to find d. We can thus plug our known variables into the last of the equations above and calculate jump height.

22 FORCE-VELOCITY PROFILING

We don't jump as high if we are carrying a load...

'Force-velocity profiling' is a method that has been popularised by the sports scientists JB Morin and Pierre Samozino. It is based upon the fact that we don't jump as high if we are carrying a load, and that the greater the load, the more our jump is affected. The method is based upon quantifying the details of the load to jump height relationship for individual athletes by measuring their jump heights under a range of different loads. This information can then be used to inform training decisions.

It does seem likely that some athletes are more badly affected by the addition of load than others. Similarly, I am sure that this information could be relevant in determining the nature of training that they need to do (and in tracking the outcome of a training protocol). Where force-velocity profiling is questionable is in suggesting that we can infer something about the force-velocity relationship from the load to jump height relationship. Unfortunately, this claim is based upon the same conflation of the force-velocity and impulse-momentum relationships as was described in the previous chapters.

An overview of the method

The basis of force-velocity profiling is to measure the jump height achieved by an athlete using a variety of loads. For each jump, the peak velocity and average force can then be calculated, which allows us to plot peak velocity and average force in a similar way to Figure 33. Hopefully, the discussion in Chapter 20 makes it clear that this is, unequivocally, not an instantaneous force-velocity relationship.

There is a further wrinkle, however. Whereas the force data presented in Figure 33 was directly measured, the average force in Morin and Samozino's method is estimated from the jump height and the displacement of the centre of mass of the athlete during the push-off phase. This brings further caveats, as I will describe shortly.

The nuts and bolts of the method

If we know a person's velocity at take-off, then we can calculate the height that the person jumps. This is because after a person leaves the ground, they can't apply any further force to themselves, and that we know that they experience a constant acceleration due to gravity. Conversely, if we know the height of a person's jump, we can calculate their velocity at take-off[*]. Thus, for any particular jump, with any particular load, if we know the

---

[*] We can calculate the height of the jump by using the equations of constant acceleration as we saw in the previous chapter. For the case that we are considering here, where the take-off velocity is the unknown that we are trying to find, the terminal velocity is 0ms⁻¹ (the peak of the jump), the acceleration is -g (gravity) and the distance travelled is the jump height, h. Using the third equation from the previous chapter we thus have:

$$0^2 = u^2 - 2gh$$

Or:

$$u = \sqrt{2gh}$$

athlete's jump height we can calculate their take-off velocity and this will be their peak velocity.

As for the average force, this can also be calculated from jump height provided we know the vertical distance moved by the athlete during the push-off. In order to calculate this we need to use the principle of conservation of mechanical energy and the work-energy relationship which we will cover in Chapter 25. In any case, the details of this calculation are not important to the argument I am making here. However, what is important to note is that to employ these equations in the way that Morin and Samozino do, we need to make the assumption that force expression is constant during the movement. In some of their writing, Morin and Samozino claim that their method does not make this assumption. This is incorrect — it is implicit in the equations that they use.

Can we predict two variables from one?

If we want to investigate the force-velocity relationship we need to treat force and velocity as two distinct variables, measure them and then look to see if they influence one another. However, in the method of Morin and Samozino we have calculated both average force and peak velocity from the height jumped by the athlete. To put this another way, our force value will determine our velocity value and vice versa. The assumptions we have made to find our force and velocity mean that they are not treated as distinct variables — rather they are entirely dependent on one another for a particular load and athlete. It is therefore unsurprising if we find a relationship between force and velocity.

To put this another way, we can't measure one variable and then expect to generate two distinct variables from it — they will always have a relationship with each other based on the influence of the original variable.

Is this really a force-velocity relationship?

If we assume that the force is constant during the push-off phase of a jump we can also calculate said force, provided we know either the time taken for the push-off, or the distance travelled by the centre of mass during the push-off. For instance, if we know the time taken for the push-off and force is constant, then the impulse accrued during the push-off will simply be the average (constant) force multiplied by time. This impulse is equal to the change in velocity as a result of the impulse-momentum relationship. Now change in velocity is equal to the take-off velocity because the velocity at the start of the push-off phase is zero. Thus we can calculate average force during the movement, as a function of take-off velocity and push-off time. In fact, Morin and Samozino derive the relationship between average force and take-off velocity using push-off distance and the work-energy relationship (which we will introduce in Chapter 25) but the argument is essentially analogous.

The method of Morin and Samozino is based upon comparing the take-off velocity with the average force, and contending that this is a force-velocity relationship. However, this is a comparison of apples and oranges. Take a look at Figure 35, which compares the actual velocity and force during a vertical jump to the model of Morin and Samozino. The question is, why choose take-off as the point for the instantaneous comparison of force and velocity – this is a purely arbitrary choice which has been justified by the fact that this is the point of peak velocity. However, one could equally choose to compare the force and velocity values at the instant of peak force, which in this example occurs at the bottom of the countermovement. Equally, one could choose to compare force and velocity values halfway through the push-off phase – you would then be comparing average velocity to average force.

Fundamentally, the problem here is that (again) the impulse-momentum relationship is being conflated with a proposed force-velocity relationship.

Figure 35. Comparison of actual height, force and velocity during the push-off phase of a vertical jump to the model of Morin and Samozino.

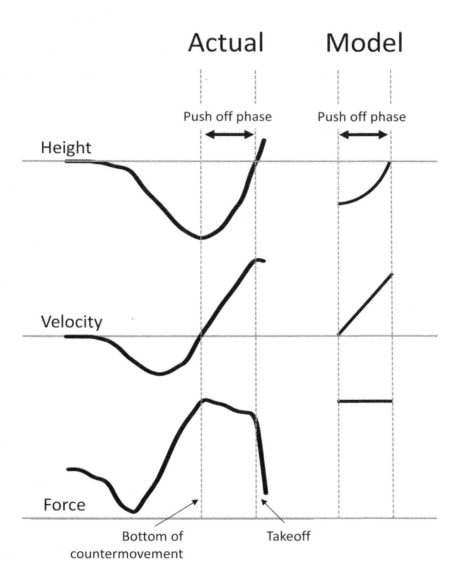

Is there value here?

To reiterate my comments at the start of this chapter, none of the arguments presented here are meant to suggest that there is not value in looking at the load to jump height relationship. I can well believe there is value in this. However, I don't believe it is correct to claim that this provides evidence for the existence of a force-velocity relationship or to suggest that the load to jump height relationship can be used as a proxy for the force-velocity relationship.

23 THE MUSCLE-TENDON UNIT

Active and passive tissue

Our muscles are active tissues. What this means is that they are able to create forces without the intervention of external actors. They are able to do this because they have a mechanism for converting chemical energy into mechanical work (and hence express force). This mechanism is the cross-bridge cycling we saw in Chapter 18. However, our muscles are not the only structures that influence the forces that are applied to our bones during movement. There are also passive tissues – tissues whose ability to exert forces is dependent on factors external to them.

How do passive tissues express forces? Essentially, when we talk about a passive tissue we are talking about a tissue that exhibits elastic behaviour. That is, if the tissue is stretched, it exerts a force that tends to return the tissue to its original state. It is easiest to visualise this by thinking of the tissue as a spring being stretched. This is handy, as the mechanics of spring behaviour are easily quantified.

Hooke's Law

The behaviour of springs is described by the eponymously named Hooke's Law[*]. Hooke's Law states that the tension (force) within a spring is directly proportional to the distance that the spring is stretched. Another way to say this is that the length change of a spring (x) is proportional to the force (F) that is applied to it:

$$F \propto x$$

To describe this relationship more formally, we introduce the variable k, the spring constant. Hooke's Law can then be written as:

$$F = kx$$

The spring constant expresses the 'stiffness' of the spring. A stiffer spring (larger k) requires more force to be stretched a given amount. As we shall see, the concept of stiffness is critically important to an understanding of athletic movement.

Hooke's Law is a very simple relationship – the degree of stretch of a spring is linearly related to the force applied. Similarly, if we are to plot the relationship on a force to length change graph, the line passes through the origin – no force means no extension.

The force-length relationship of passive tissue

Unfortunately, the behaviour of the passive tissue within muscle is not entirely 'Hookeian'. Although there is a part of the length-tension curve

---

[*] Robert Hooke was a contemporary of Isaac Newton. The two had a famously acrimonious relationship. In fact, some commentators have interpreted Newton's famous quote about standing on the shoulders of giants ("if I have seen further it is by standing on the shoulders of giants") as a gibe at Hooke's height.

that is somewhat linear, the curve as a whole is decidedly non-linear (Figure 36). However, in common physiological ranges if we envisage the passive behaviour of muscle as being somewhat like an elastic band we are probably OK. The only other thing to be aware of is that muscle will only start expressing force passively if it is stretched above its resting length.

Figure 36. Length-tension relationship of passive tissue.

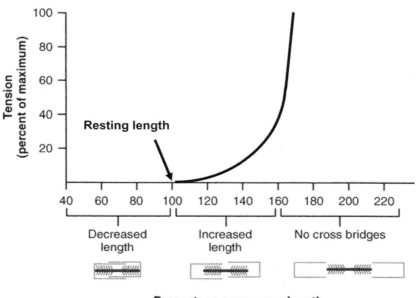

Percentage sarcomere length

The muscle-tendon unit

We are now in a position where we can start to think in more detail about the way in which forces are applied to bones. In order to do so, we need to introduce the concept of a 'muscle-tendon' unit. This is because muscle fibres don't exist in isolation but are rather part of system that also includes passive tissues. Firstly, muscles are attached to bones by tendons. Secondly, connective tissues that exhibit elastic behaviour are found between muscle fibres. A typical model of a muscle-tendon unit is given in Figure 37.

Figure 37. The muscle-tendon unit[11]. The contractile (CE) and passive elements (PE) of the muscle tissue are at an angle α to the tendon. L^T, L^{MT} and L^M are the lengths of the tendon, muscle and muscle-tendon unit respectively. F^T and F^M are the forces in the tendon and muscle.

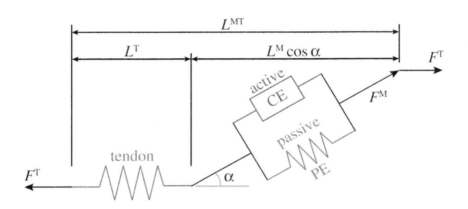

Figure 38. Length-tension relationship of the muscle-tendon unit.

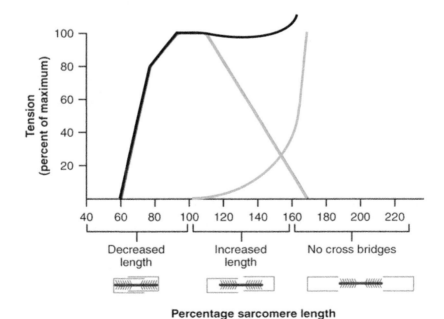

The length-tension relationship of the complete muscle-tendon unit is thus a combination of the properties of the active and passive tissues. Figure 38 is a combination of Figures 30 and 36 and illustrates this relationship.

Why?

The length-tension relationship shown in Figure 38 is complex and highly non-linear. Equally, we can create similar forces using different combinations of the active and passive tissue. This then begs the question: why?

One of the main reasons for this is that, as we have seen, the active generation of force by the contractile tissue takes time. In contrast, when a passive tissue is stretched force expression will be immediate. For this reason, one mechanism which our bodies often use to express force is the so called stretch-shortening cycle. This is where a muscle-tendon unit goes through a cycle of eccentric, isometric and concentric contractions – that is, the muscle-tendon unit is first stretched and then shortens. This both increases the maximum level of force that can be reached and increases the rate of force development. There are a few different neural mechanisms and reflexes which assist in this process.

The other advantage of this arrangement is that it lends flexibility to the musculoskeletal system. As there are a range of ways that we can express force it gives us more options for the way that we move.

Again, an understanding of what is going on at the muscle-tendon unit level is important when we programme training. For instance, we can target our training interventions to different parts of the muscle-tendon unit. Equally, training that improves our ability to employ the stretch-shortening cycle can have a profound effect on performance.

24 STIFFNESS AND FLEXIBILITY

What are we talking about?

Stiffness is one of the most ambiguous concepts in strength and conditioning. Depending on the context, sometimes stiffness seems desirable, and at other times it is a BAD thing. Sometimes increasing our stiffness is a training goal (e.g. plyometrics), whereas at other times we are trying to decrease it (e.g. stretching). How can this be?

Well again, the source of the confusion is terminology. What is stiff and when?

Stiffness versus flexibility

The best place to start is to be very clear what we are talking about when we refer to stiffness. For the purposes of this discussion when I refer to stiffness I am talking about the behaviour of the musculoskeletal system when muscles and tendons are being lengthened by the application of external force. We are thus thinking about the spring-like behaviour of tissues, joints and limbs. In particular, we can define stiffness as the change in length when a given force is applied. This relationship can be modelled by Hooke's Law in which case the spring constant describes the stiffness of the system.

One critical factor that it is important to understand is that the stiffness of our muscle-tendon units and joints is very manipulable. In particular, we have a fantastic capability to stiffen or relax our bodies to meet the demands of the task facing us. It would thus be an error to treat the stiffness of our bodies as some type of immutable characteristic. This ability is provided by the active nature of muscle contraction as the material properties of some tissues (e.g. tendons and bones) are largely constant acutely (although can be altered through training).

As a general term, flexibility describes the ease with which a material can be bent and then return to its original shape. However, in human performance terms, flexibility is generally used to describe how easy it is to passively move a person's joints – particularly near the end of their range of motion. One factor in this is clearly the stiffness of a person's muscles. When we are fatigued the day after intense activity we will often describe ourselves as being stiff, and in this case we are describing the fact that we have a decrease in our flexibility. However, it is important to recognise that the stiffness of our muscles is only one factor that determines the full range of motion of our joints. An athlete can have a very large range of motion, but still have the ability to make themselves very stiff when the occasion demands.

What body part?

Probably the most critical thing to specify when we are talking about stiffness is the part of the body in question. In particular, as the body is made up of individual tissues, joints, limbs etc, to what structural level are we referring. When we talk about stiffness we could be referring to the properties of a particular tissue (i.e. how stiff is the Achilles tendon), a specific muscle tendon unit, the behaviour of a joint or the behaviour of a whole limb. Similarly, we need to think about whether the stiffness we are referring to is a description of purely the mechanical properties of a structure, or whether we are also including the way in which its behaviour is controlled and mediated by the action of the nervous system.

Tendon

In terms of the tendon, let's consider two different force production scenarios. Firstly, if the muscle-tendon unit is producing force primarily by active shortening of the muscle (a concentric action), then the role of the tendon is to transmit that force to the bones. In this case, we probably want the tendon to act like an inextensible string, so that the full force (and length change) is transmitted to the bone. This means that we would want the tendon to be very stiff. Secondly, if the muscle is acting isometrically and not changing length, but the joint is being flexed or extended, then the tendon will be being stretched (think high speed running or bouncing). In this case, elastic energy is being stored in the tendon to be used to facilitate joint extension. Stiffer springs are better at storing and returning elastic energy so again, we would want a stiffer tendon. There is a point of diminishing returns, however, as we still need to be able to stretch the tendon and thus the optimal stiffness will be dependent on our strength capabilities and the forces that we tend to experience during movement.

Muscle

Whereas the stiffness of the tendon is purely a function of its mechanical properties, the same is not true of muscle. Instead we have both the passive and contractile elements to consider. In particular, the stiffness of the contractile element will depend on its activation. We'll exemplify the range of considerations by considering the case where we are simply trying to lengthen the muscle as much as possible, both acutely and through training.

Acutely, the degree to which we can stretch the contractile element depends on a range of factors. This is because the muscle is under our nervous system control as well as being influenced by a range of mechanoreceptors*.

---

* There are two mechanoreceptors of particular importance. The Golgi tendon organ will tend to inhibit the force production capability of the contractile element

Our ability to allow our muscles to be stretched is thus dependent on a range of factors which include our psychological ability to be able to relax and the speed of the stretch. If we want to improve our ability to allow our muscles to be stretched then an important aspect is training our nervous system to stay calm when our muscles are stretched.

Of course, there are also material factors that affect the ability of a person to stretch their muscles. In particular, if a given muscle has more sarcomeres in series then its resting length will be greater. Similarly, all things being equal, a muscle with more sarcomeres in series will stretch more when subjected to a given force*. However, this does not mean that an athlete with longer muscles will necessarily be less stiff, as the stiffness is both a function of the behaviour of the sarcomeres and the number of sarcomeres in parallel (the muscle cross-sectional area). It is worth emphasising the meaning of this – an athlete can be both flexible and stiff. They are not mutually exclusive.

Muscle-tendon units, joints and limbs

As we saw in the previous chapter, the muscle-tendon unit is comprised of passive and active elements. Clearly, the behaviour of the muscle-tendon unit will depend on the properties of its components but at the same time, its behaviour is influenced by the relative involvement of different tissues within a given task, which is in itself determined by the nervous system. Using the broadest possible generalisation, the more strongly we activate the muscle during an eccentric muscle action, the more we will stretch the tendon during the action. In doing so, we will shift the behaviour of the muscle-tendon unit towards the elastic regime, and its stiffness will increasingly be a consequence of the material properties of the tendon. As the flexion/extension of the joints is governed by the behaviour of the

---

if the tension in the muscle-tendon unit exceeds a certain amount. In contrast, muscle spindles will tend to increase muscle force if the speed of stretch of a muscle is too great.

* This can be understood by thinking of a chain of springs in series. As the same force will act on each spring, each spring will extend by the same amount. More springs equals more extension.

muscle-tendon units, and the behaviour of a limb is determined by the behaviour of the joints, we can broadly think of the limb being able to regulate stiffness in a similar fashion to the muscle-tendon unit.

We are thus able to regulate the stiffness of our limbs based on the task in hand. For instance, we can stiffen our lower limb and use it like a stiff spring in an activity like high speed running. Alternatively, we can make it much less stiff in order to cushion the forces that we experience when landing after a vertical jump. What this means is that one of our training considerations is to think about the desired stiffness behaviour of the limb during the sport skill in question.

Equally, it should be emphasised that being flexible does not preclude us from being stiff. Of course, a training modality like static stretching might compromise our ability to stiffen the lower limb by changing the material properties of our elastic tissues. However, this is not inevitable and we can improve our range of motion while still maintaining or even improving the stiffness capacities of our bodies.

25 ENERGY

Total force: A recap

All the way back in Chapter 3, we saw that when we want to analyse movement it is helpful to have some measure of total force. In this book we have seen two ways of measuring total force, impulse and work done. So far, we have mainly focused on impulse, because the impulse-momentum relationship tells us that the net impulse applied will be related to the change in velocity and that often in sport change in velocity during a movement skill is a key parameter. However, there are situations where work done is a more useful variable. This is because there is a relationship between work and energy that is somewhat analogous to the impulse-momentum relationship.

First of all, let's revise the meaning of impulse and work. Impulse is the sum of the force expressed with respect to time. It is the area underneath the force-time curve. In contrast, work done is the sum of the force expressed with respect to distance (or strictly displacement). It is the area under the force-distance curve (Figure 39).

Figure 39. Force-time and force-distance curves for jumping.

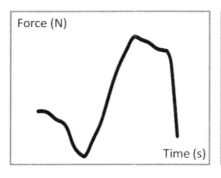 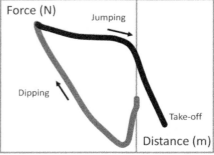

Mathematically, we define impulse and work as follows:

$$I = \int F\, dt \qquad\qquad W = \int F\, dx$$

It is clear to see how work is analogous to impulse. Now, in this book we have relied heavily on the impulse-momentum relationship. Is there an analogous relationship for work?

Work-energy relationship

In short, yes! The work-energy relationship can be derived from Newton's 2nd Law in exactly the same way as the impulse-momentum relationship just focussing on displacement rather than time*:

---

* I provide the derivation of this relationship below. It requires some understanding of calculus so please don't worry if you can't follow it exactly – the point here is mainly to just show that the relationship is derived directly from Newton's 2nd Law.

Firstly, let's consider a mass that is being accelerated by a force. Newton's 2nd Law gives us the relationship between this force and the acceleration. However, if the mass is on Earth it will also have the force of gravity acting on it (mg) thus we have:

$$W = \frac{1}{2}m \times \Delta(v^2) + mg \times \Delta x$$

At first glance, this seems like quite a complicated expression, but it breaks down quite simply. The first part of the right hand side of the equation

---

$$F = ma + mg$$

If I take the integral with respect to x on each side:

$$\int F\,dx = \int ma\,dx + \int mg\,dx$$

We can recognise that the left hand side of the equation is simply the work done, and that acceleration is the derivative of velocity. We can also take the mass and gravity terms outside of the integral sign as they are constants:

$$W = m\int \frac{dv}{dt}dx + mg\int dx$$

We can now solve the second integral on the right hand side, and make a handy substitution in the first integral:

$$W = m\int \frac{dv}{dx} \times \frac{dx}{dt}dx + mgx$$

Cancelling the dx terms with each other and rearranging within the first integral:

$$W = m\int \frac{dx}{dt}dv + mgx$$

Now the derivative of x is velocity:

$$W = m\int v\,dv + mgx$$

Finally, we can solve the first integral, and we have derived the work-energy relationship:

$$W = \frac{1}{2}m \times \Delta(v^2) + mg \times \Delta x$$

represents the energy that an object has due to the fact that it is moving - its kinetic energy (E_k).

$$E_k = \frac{1}{2}mv^2$$

We can gain an intuitive understanding of the meaning of kinetic energy by considering an object colliding with a wall. If the object has more energy, it will do more damage to the wall. Considering the formula, clearly a heavier object will do more damage, however this is a linear relationship. In contrast, as kinetic energy is proportional to velocity squared, increases in velocity have an immense effect on the amount of damage inflicted. This can help us understand why guns are so destructive – although bullets have very little mass they travel at very high velocities.

Similarly, the second part of the right hand side represents the potential energy (E_p) – that is, the energy that an object has based on its elevation above the surface of the Earth.

$$E_p = mgx$$

Again, an intuitive understanding can be gained by considering an object that is dropped onto the ground. If the object is heavier it will do more damage, as there is a linear relationship between energy and mass. Equally, if the object is dropped from a greater height it will also do more damage, and the relationship between height and energy is also linear.

The work-energy relationship therefore allows us to give a mechanical definition of what 'energy' actually is. When we do work on an object, we increase its energy. Therefore, the energy of an object represents the net amount of work done on that object.

Conservation of energy

Continuing the analogy with impulse, just as momentum is conserved*, so is energy. What this means is that the total energy of a system stays the same unless work is done on the system. Let's illustrate this by considering what happens during an Olympic-style snatch. When the barbell is resting on the floor it has no kinetic energy as it is not moving, and it has no potential energy as it is on the ground. The lifter then does work on the barbell (applying force to it as they displace it overhead). At the end of the lift, the lifter will be holding the barbell stationary overhead. The barbell now has a potential energy that is equal to the amount of work that has been done on it and that is determined by the mass of the barbell and its height above the ground.

When the athlete drops the barbell, it starts to lose potential energy commensurate with its drop in height. However, the principle of conservation of energy says that energy can't be lost, so where does this energy go? Well, as the barbell falls it gains velocity, and thus gains kinetic energy. The potential energy is therefore converted to kinetic energy, and at the point that the barbell reaches the floor, all of the potential energy has now been converted into kinetic energy.

Finally, when the barbell collides with the floor its velocity is rapidly brought to zero, and thus the barbell now has zero energy again. How can this be? Well, during the collision, substantial forces are impressed upon the barbell by the floor – that is, negative work is done on the barbell, decreasing its energy.

A role for power!

In sports like cycling and rowing it is common for performances to be quantified in terms of the power output. I think this makes a lot of sense if considered in light of the work-energy relationship. Performance in

---

* That is, the momentum of a system stays the same unless an external force is applied to it.

endurance sports is predicated on the athlete's ability to access energy. The ability to access energy is generally measured using physiological means. For instance, we often measure an athlete's aerobic capacity by measuring their ability to use oxygen. If an athlete uses more oxygen it means that they are able to generate more chemical energy to power their movement. When an athlete moves they convert chemical energy into mechanical work. The more chemical energy they can access in a given time frame, the more work they are able to perform in that time frame. The amount of work they are able to do per unit time is represented by their power output. Thus there is a clear link between energy expended and power output and thus for endurance sports power is a very useful measure.

26 FORCE ABSORPTION?

Force cannot be absorbed!

It is very common to hear coaches talk about force absorption strategies or training for the ability to absorb force. However, force is not a quality that can be absorbed. This is a direct consequence of Newton's 3rd Law. If an object exerts a force upon us, we in turn exert the same force back on it. We do this by producing, not absorbing, forces (within our muscle-tendon units).

Understanding the eccentric regime

When people talk about absorbing forces they are typically talking about what happens during eccentric muscle actions, when muscles are lengthening under high external forces. It is most common to see force absorption talked about in the context of landing, deceleration or change of direction. These activities do require athletes to cope with large external forces and some athletes are clearly better able to handle high forces than others. This ability is important as it can have both injury and performance implications. However, effective training strategies require a better understanding of the mechanism by which we handle high external forces – as force is not absorbed it is not possible to train this ability.

Landing

For the purposes of the discussion in this chapter, let's consider an athlete landing after a vertical jump. When the athlete makes contact with the floor they will have a vertical velocity downwards that is determined by the height they jumped (the higher they jumped, the higher their velocity when they hit the ground). The landing task is to bring that velocity to zero by applying force to the ground.

In order to analyse this situation we need to use the impulse-momentum relationship:

$$I = \mathrm{m} \times \Delta v$$

The athlete's change in momentum as they land will be equal to the impulse that they apply. Now remember that impulse is the area underneath the force-time curve, and so is a function of force and time. We can then use this to understand the options available to our athlete.

Force reduction strategy

In the context of landing, one 'force absorption' strategy is to change our landing mechanics. This generally equates to having a greater amount of ankle, knee and hip flexion during landing. Now, the effect of having a greater joint excursion during landing is typically to prolong the length of the landing phase – i.e. force is exerted for longer. What this means is that the athlete will have to produce a lower mean force in order to impress the impulse that is required for the landing. Therefore, this is not a force absorption strategy, it is force reduction.

Force reduction strategies will clearly help an athlete who is struggling to cope with high forces during eccentric actions, as they can moderate the force requirements of the task to bring them within their own force production capabilities. Similarly, a reduction of the force demands imposed on the musculoskeletal system will reduce injury risk.

Force capacity strategy

Of course, the increase in the time taken for the landing manoeuvre may be undesirable in some sporting contexts. The other possible avenue we have to improve our ability to handle high external forces is simply to improve our capacity for exerting force and condition our tissues to tolerate higher forces. Not only will an improved ability to tolerate higher forces allow the time of a manoeuvre to be minimised, but it might also allow the storage and reuse of more elastic energy as we will see shortly.

Work-energy relationship

We can also gain insight into the eccentric regime if we consider the work-energy relationship. When the athlete is at the peak of their vertical jump they have a potential energy that is determined by the height of their centre of mass above the ground*. When they come to rest after completing the landing their potential energy will have decreased due to the loss of height of their centre of mass. The landing thus represents a decrease in energy. The principle of conservation of energy tells us that the energy in the system can only change if we do work on the system. The landing can therefore be characterised as us performing negative work on our centre of mass. Again, this should make sense – the force is being applied in the opposite direction to the movement of the centre of mass.

Where does this energy go? Is it absorbed? Well not really – it is more accurate to describe it as being dissipated into the environment in the form of noise, heat, etc.

Is anything absorbed?

As usual, in order to answer this question I guess it is first important to understand what we mean by absorbed. I will use an analogy – when a sponge absorbs water it means it is taken into the material of the sponge,

---

* Their kinetic energy is zero as they have zero velocity at the peak of their jump.

but can then be recovered by squeezing the sponge. Does anything resemble this during landing or other eccentric activities?

The answer to this is probably yes. At least in some scenarios we have the potential to store and reuse elastic energy. Let's say that after landing an athlete tries to bounce off the floor as quickly as they can (as seen in a drop jump off a box). In this case, some of the potential energy that the athlete loses as they fall can be used to stretch the tendons eccentrically. When a spring is stretched, energy is stored, which can then be recovered when the spring is allowed to recoil. Thus, some of the potential energy that the athlete had at the peak of their jump can be 'absorbed' as strain energy*.

There are some important limitations to the storage and reuse of elastic energy. The first is that energy stored in this way dissipates very quickly, and so this type of 'absorption' is only seen in activities that have short ground contact times like sprinting or drop jumping. This is why 'true' plyometrics are defined to be activities with short contact times. The second is that stiffer tendons are more efficient at storing elastic energy as less energy is lost to hysteresis. However, in order to stretch a stiffer tendon the athlete will need to be stronger.

---

* More correctly, as the athlete falls their potential energy is converted to kinetic energy (as their velocity increases). Once the athlete makes contact with the floor, some of this kinetic energy is converted to strain energy and the rest is dissipated by the negative work performed by the athlete.

CONCLUSION

From understanding force we can achieve enlightenment...

The heading of this sub-section is the quote that prefaced this book. It is a bold claim...

What I hope is that I have convinced you that one of the most critical goals of training is to improve our ability to express force within the sporting environment. This can be a forbidding task as the production of force by our bodies is far from simple and we have a range of different strategies that we can use. If we want to train in a 'specific' way, we need to try and understand the particular force production strategies that are used in our athlete's sport and then choose training activities that are targeted at those strategies.

In Chapter 9, I presented a modified version of the dynamic correspondence criteria first popularised in the West by Siff and Verkhoshansky. I suggested that first and foremost we need to make sure that the training activities we choose satisfy the fundamental training principle of providing the possibility for overload or variation (in terms of force and/or impulse production). If this first criterion is met, I then suggested it was important to consider the way in which force is produced.

This can then allow us to choose training activities that enhance force expression in the sporting activity at hand. This involves a consideration of the gross movement strategy used by the athlete (push, pull, bounce or block), their body position, and the way in which force is generated at the level of the muscle-tendon unit.

Along the way we have taken a look at a number of theories that are popular in the training literature. Most of these contain some elements of truth but are compromised by a desire to present a system that is intuitively appealing. This tends to obscure the mechanics and makes the link between training and force production less obvious. They conceal rather than enlighten.

FIGURE LICENSES AND ATTRIBUTIONS

1. The photo is in the public domain and was distributed by maxpixel.net under the terms of the Creative Commons Zero license CC0.

2. Image is in the public domain.

3. Image is in the public domain.

4. Screenshots taken from https://youtu.be/qN3apht8zRs (@LocomotorLabSMU). Thanks to Professor Peter Weyand for providing permission to use these images.

5. Thanks to Stuart McMillan (Twitter: @StuartMcMillan1) for providing the image.

6. Drawing of the musculoskeletal anatomy of the feline limb is in the public domain.

7. A is reproduced under the terms of the Creative Commons Attribution 4.0 International license. It is taken from the OpenStax Anatomy and Physiology Textbook and has been recoloured. B is reproduced under the terms of the Creative Commons Attribution 2.5 Generic license. It is taken from Tskhovrebova and Trinick (2012) and has been cropped, recoloured and relabelled.

    https://creativecommons.org/licenses/by/4.0/legalcode
    https://openstax.org/details/books/anatomy-and-physiology
    https://creativecommons.org/licenses/by/2.5/legalcode

    Tskhovrebova, L., & Trinick, J. (2012). Making muscle elastic: The structural basis of myomesin stretching. *PLoS Biology, 10*, e1001264.

8. The figure is reproduced under the terms of the Creative Commons Attribution-Share Alike 3.0 Unported license. It is taken from Richfield (2014) and has been recoloured.

    https://creativecommons.org/licenses/by-sa/3.0/legalcode

    Richfield, D. (2014). Medical gallery of David Richfield. *Wikijournal of Medicine, 1*.

9. The figure is reproduced under the terms of the Creative Commons Attribution 4.0 International license. It is taken from CNX Openstax Biology and has been cropped, edited and recoloured.

    https://creativecommons.org/licenses/by/4.0/legalcode
    https://openstax.org/books/biology-2e/pages/1-introduction

10. The figure is reproduced under the terms of the Creative Commons Attribution 4.0 International license. It is taken from Openstax Anatomy and Physiology and has been recoloured.

    https://creativecommons.org/licenses/by/4.0/legalcode
    https://openstax.org/books/anatomy-and-physiology/pages/1-introduction

11. The figure is reproduced under the terms of the Creative Commons Attribution 4.0 International license. It is taken from Hu et al. (2017) and has been cropped, recoloured and relabelled.

    https://creativecommons.org/licenses/by/4.0/legalcode

    Hu, X., Charles, J. P., Akay, T., Hutchinson, J. R., & Blemker, S. S. (2017). Are mice good models for human neuromuscular disease ? Comparing muscle excursions in walking between mice and humans. *Skeletal Muscle, 7,* 26.

12. Data is taken from:

    Cormie, P., McCaulley, G. O., Triplett, N. T., & McBride, J. M. (2007). Optimal loading for maximal power output during lower-body resistance exercises. *Medicine and Science in Sports and Exercise, 39,* 340-349.

ABOUT THE AUTHOR

Dan is a Reader in Strength and Conditioning and Programme Director of the MSc in Strength and Conditioning at St Mary's University, Twickenham, UK. Before joining St Mary's he was employed as a strength and conditioning coach at the English Institute of Sport where he worked with World and Olympic champions in track and field athletics, rowing, canoeing and rugby. Dan's PhD is in biomedical engineering (from Imperial College London) and his research interests include musculoskeletal modelling, functional anatomy and strength training. He has published around 60 articles in peer reviewed scientific and professional practice journals. He is a founder member of the UK Strength and Conditioning Association and currently serves the organisation as Director of Finance and Administration (a post he also held between 2005 and 2009). He lives in the Czech Republic with his wife, three children and two cats.

Printed in Great Britain
by Amazon

BURMA

A SOLDIER'S CAMPAIGN
IN 20 OBJECTS

David Meara

DAVID MEARA

AMBERLEY

In loving memory of John and Audrey Alexander

Restaurant, Myingyan, 22 December 1942.

First published 2022

Amberley Publishing
The Hill, Stroud
Gloucestershire, GL5 4EP

www.amberley-books.com

British Library Cataloguing in Publication Data.
A catalogue record for this book is available from the British Library.

ISBN 978 1 3981 0580 5 (print)
ISBN 978 1 3981 0581 2 (ebook)

Typesetting by SJmagic DESIGN SERVICES, India.
Printed in Great Britain.

Contents

LIST OF TWENTY OBJECTS

1. Japanese Imperial Saving Book.
2. British Army Warrant Book.
3. Japanese Family Photographs.
4. History of the 17th Indian Division.
5. John Alexander's Uniform, Equipment and Insignia.
6. Japanese Postcards and Letter Cards.
7. Burmese Knife.
8. Japanese Coloured Sketches.
9. Japanese Officers' Swords.
10. Japanese Good Luck Flags.
11. Japanese Uniform Insignia.
12. John Alexander's Service Diary.
13. The Black Cat Badge.
14. Kooa Cigarettes.
15 Japanese Rifle Ammunition and Knife.
16. Japanese Ivory Chopsticks.
17. The Elephant Bandoola.

18. Japanese Invasion Money.
19. Postcards Home.
20. Burmese Sapphire Rings.

Chef Sori, Myingyan, 31 May 1942.

Preface and Acknowledgements

It is now over seventy-five years since the end of the Second World War with the defeat of the Japanese and their surrender following the bombing of Hiroshima and Nagasaki. The few remaining veterans of the war in Burma and the Pacific are now old, and when they die their memories will go with them. Soon we shall only be able to experience those battles through books, films and exhibits in museums. I believe it is important that we continue to honour the memory of those who fought and died for their country, and to explain these far distant conflicts to younger generations for whom it must all seem like ancient history. One powerful way to make that connection is through the objects associated with the war in the Far East which those who fought there left behind or brought home with them. By chance my father-in-law, John Alexander, brought back just such a disparate collection of objects, and I decided to use these as the focus for this account of the Burma Campaign.

Having decided to do so, I was faced with the challenge of weaving them into an orderly narrative to give the book a coherent structure. I also had to try to puzzle out how to interpret some of the objects and translate the Japanese writing. I am very grateful to Timothy Meara for the original idea for the book; to Clare Pollard of the Ashmolean Museum, Oxford, for help and advice; to Hisako Bremner for her painstaking translation work; to Bob Cook, the Curator of the Kohima Museum at Imphal Barracks, York, for background information; to Martin Slivka for his photography of some of the objects illustrated in the book; and to Sophie Fisher and the Imperial War Museum for use of their archive of photographs of the Burma Campaign.

I am grateful to my brother-in-law, David Alexander, for generously sharing the family archive material in his possession, together with items belonging to his father that form part of the collection of twenty objects, and also to my daughter Susie Hettige for lending me some other items belonging to her grandfather in her possession.

I would like to thank Charles and Beverly Leach for sending me information and pictures relating to Charles' uncle, Geoffrey Hayward, who also served in the Royal Engineers; to Joyce and Leslie Howard for permission to use the reminiscences of Joyce's father John Tulloch; and to Chris and Robert Pearce for lending me material about the campaign which belonged to Chris's father, George Feasey. I would also like to express my gratitude to Tracey Salt for typing and retyping my manuscript, patiently deciphering my handwriting, and saving me from numerous errors. Above all I would like to express my love and admiration for John and Audrey Alexander, my parents-in-law, who, like so many of their generation, sacrificed some of the best years of their lives to support and defend their country in its time of gravest need, and who lived to rebuild their lives and see their family grow and flourish. To Rosemary, their daughter, I express my profound gratitude for her love and support.

It is my hope that in telling the story of the Burma Campaign through this diverse collection of objects, we can discover some personal connection and humanity in that most inhumane of human conflicts.

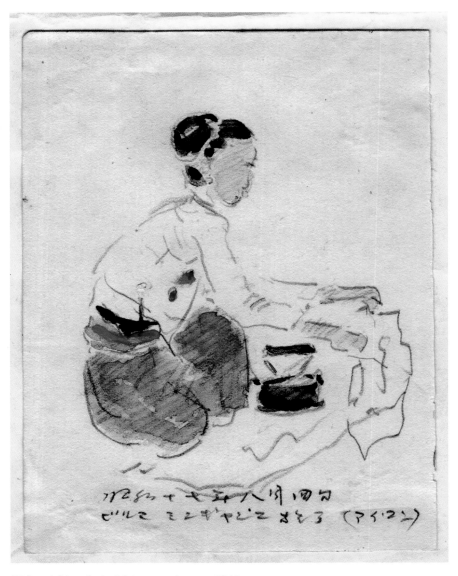

Girl weighing fruit, Myingyan, August 1942.

Chapter I

Souvenirs of War

Just over a fortnight after VE Day 1945, which marked the end of the war in Europe, a small exhibition opened in Reigate, Surrey, at the National Savings Centre in the High Street. The exhibition consisted of a window display of Japanese war souvenirs brought back from Burma by an officer in the Royal Engineers who lived locally, Captain John Willis Alexander. He had fought in 60 Indian Light Field Company, The Queen Victoria's Own Madras Sappers and Miners, in the 17th Indian Division of the XIVth Army throughout the Burma Campaign, and had come home on leave.

As many returning soldiers did, he brought back a varied assortment of objects, taken from Japanese soldiers, including a sword, knives, flags, rifle ammunition, chopsticks, cigarettes, money, photographs and coloured sketches. One object that was highlighted in the exhibition was an Imperial Savings Book belonging to a Japanese soldier, duly entered with the amount and date of his deposits, 'the security of which would not appear to compare favourably with investments in British Savings.', as the caption complacently pointed out. The aims of the exhibition were both to highlight the importance of continuing to support the War Savings Campaign at home ('Over £7,500,000 has already been saved in the Borough of Reigate'), and to remind the population that although the war had been won in Europe, the campaign against the

Major John Willis Alexander, Royal Engineers.
(Author's collection)

Japanese in Burma was still being waged, and local support was therefore still needed. The National Savings Campaign had been set up by the War Office in November 1939, operating through Regional and Local Savings Committees, to raise money for the purchase of weaponry such as aeroplanes and tanks for the war effort. A notice in the Reigate window display announced:

> The fact that Japanese soldiers carry their Savings Books with them on active service reminds us that the people of Japan have not yet given up hope of ultimate victory and are sparing no effort to accomplish that purpose. If we wish to prove them wrong in the shortest possible time we must prove that we are better fighters and better SAVERS.

One wonders what the inhabitants of Reigate made of this random collection of objects relating to a campaign in a country about which they knew little, especially as hostilities in the main theatres of war had been concluded, and the British population was beginning to think about the possibility of peace in a post-war world. The campaign in Burma is often described as 'The Forgotten War' and the soldiers who fought in it as 'The Forgotten Army'. This was partly because the campaign was fought in a far-off place, on the other side of the world, and partly because the XIVth Army was largely made up of Indian Divisions, Gurkhas, West African Divisions, and Australian and New Zealand troops – all drawn willingly from the vast resources of the British Empire. But this very diversity perhaps made the war in Burma seem remote to the people of Britain. At the time the Prime Minister Winston Churchill had another reason for keeping the campaign out of the public eye, certainly during late 1943 when he wanted the focus to be on the campaign in Italy in which the Americans had invested four divisions. 'It would be better if it were forgotten', Churchill is reported to have said, although as the war in the Mediterranean achieved success during 1944, he was once again happy to highlight the turning tide of the Allies' fortunes in Burma.

From the truly multinational troops of the XIVth Army many stories emerge of courage, cruelty, heroism and audacity in the course of the campaign, and many thousands of Allied and Japanese soldiers lost their lives in the jungles, plains, mountains and river valleys of Burma. As well as his souvenirs, Captain John Alexander came back home with vivid and terrible memories of the things he had seen and done on the field of battle.

After the exhibition in Reigate and his eventual demobilisation from the army he stored away his collection of objects together with his army uniform, bivouac tent and other military equipment in his service trunk, and forgot about them, but the memories, and the nightmares, remained. He was in fact suffering from what we now know to be Post Traumatic Stress Disorder (PTSD), a condition that wasn't recognised or treated at the time. For most of the rest of his life he suffered from recurrent nightmares, patiently and lovingly helped and supported by his wife Audrey, who taught him to knit to help alleviate his condition.

John Alexander (1921–2010) was my father-in-law, and although I knew him for nearly fifty years, he never talked about his wartime experiences. On the one occasion when his son tried to record some reminiscences of their lives in wartime, John spoke briefly about Burma, and Audrey about her time in the W.R.N.S., before Audrey cut the interview short, with the comment, 'And now let's talk of happier things.' This unwillingness to recall or dwell on wartime experiences, so common among those who endured the trauma of the Second World War, meant that many details of what John and others did during the Burma Campaign have been lost. But his interesting collection of objects, stowed away in his attic, and now passed down to his son and grandson, remains as mute testimony to that often-forgotten conflict in a far-off land.

Many accounts of the Burma Campaign have been published, notably Field Marshal Sir William Slim's *Defeat into Victory* (1956), the official history of *The War Against Japan* (HMSO Vols. I–IV), the *Imperial War Museum Book of the War in Burma* (2002), and numerous other books covering specific parts of the campaign or individual experiences. For a soldier's view of the final months of the campaign you can't do better than *Quartered Safe Out Here* by George MacDonald Frazer (Harper, 2000). It describes the push for Rangoon by Nine Section, a group of Cumbrian Borderers in the 17th Indian Division, and gives a view of the unfolding action which doesn't usually appear in the official military histories. I have made extensive use of the excellent account written by Lieutenant-Colonel Frank Owen OBE and published by The Central Office of Information for South-East Asia Command in 1946 (HMSO). It is at times somewhat 'gung-ho' in its outlook, but it gives a good idea of what the campaign felt like on the ground, and was written soon after the events it recorded.

All of these books give detailed accounts of the various theatres of war and the battles on the various fronts, and it is therefore not my intention to repeat what has already been very fully covered and explained, although I shall try to give the reader an idea of the general flow of the conflict and an outline of what was a complex and frequently confusing campaign. Into that narrative I have inserted the objects my father-in-law brought back, to try to get behind the bare bones of military strategy and conjure up something of the personal experience of those who took part as soldiers on both sides, both British and Japanese.

This collection of artefacts, random survivals from past history, offers us a way of touching past lives, and carries messages about the people who owned and used them, and about the places they came from and passed through. As the British author D. H. Lawrence wrote:

Things men have made with wakened hands and put soft life into
Are awake through years with transferred touch, and go on glowing for long years.
And for this reason, some old things are lovely,
Warm still with the life of forgotten men who made them.

This thought taps into a feeling that is latent in contemporary culture, that objects are or have become the past they narrate, and so bring both the object and the narrative of the past much closer to our eyes. The enormous success of the British Museum's exhibition A History of the World in 100 Objects in 2010, curated by Neil MacGregor, has encouraged us to wake up to the value of 'object lessons', and has given me the idea of telling the story of the Burma Campaign in a slightly different way, in an attempt to get beyond the often repeated details of military tactics and strategy. Because their random nature makes it difficult to create a narrative from this collection of objects alone, I have framed the book around a chronological account of the campaign, focusing on the story of the 17th Indian Division, known as 'The Black Cats', in which my father-in-law served, and which was probably the most famous Indian Division to serve in the East. They arrived in Burma at the beginning of the campaign, and remained on active duty until after the end of the war. Two other individuals appear briefly in the narrative: Geoffrey Hayward, who was a Quartermaster Sergeant in the Royal Engineers, and

Geoffrey Hayward, RE, and friends at the training camp at Kirkee, Poona, on his arrival in India in January 1942. He is standing in the middle at the back. He was soon posted to 110 Company, RE, in north-eastern Assam. (Charles and Beverly Leach)

John Tulloch, a Wireless Operator in the RAF. The other person who appears in this story is Shoichi Yoshida, who may have been a Second Lieutenant in the Japanese 33rd Army, because a number of the objects which John brought back may have belonged to him. There are only two objects in the collection that can be assigned to a specific individual, the two 'good luck' flags, both of which bear the name 'Shoichi Yoshida'. It is impossible to know whether the majority of the objects came from one soldier, or from a number of soldiers. Apart from the swords, they would almost certainly have been taken from dead soldiers on the battlefield. Because of the Japanese military mindset, the vast majority of Japanese troops were killed in battle or took their own lives. Very few soldiers surrendered or allowed themselves to be captured. It became an accepted thing for Allied soldiers, when checking bodies, to take items as souvenirs of war, as soldiers have done since ancient times. The main motive seems to have been to bring back mementoes of their time at war, a reminder to themselves and others that they had participated in an extraordinary and perilous event and lived to tell the tale. As the old saying goes, 'To the victor belong the spoils'. Today we may find this distasteful, but young soldiers at the time were eager for souvenirs and felt it was acceptable to take personal items from those who had fallen on the field of battle. Whatever our contemporary view of such artefacts may be, this collection of objects, which belonged to soldiers on both sides of the conflict, offers a way into this distant campaign and a tangible and personal connection to those who spent four years of their young lives in a theatre of war that must have seemed strange and remote to them all.

Objects: 1. Japanese Savings Book, 2. Geoffrey Hayward Warrant Book, 3. Japanese Family Photos.

1. JAPANESE IMPERIAL SAVINGS BOOK

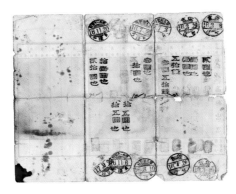

After their occupation of territories in South-East Asia one of Japan's first acts was to revalue the yen and fix a unit of currency in each of the occupied countries equivalent to one yen. This resulted in the yen gaining in value, and goods from South-East Asia becoming cheaper for Japan to purchase and import. The creation of the Greater East Asia Co-Prosperity Sphere was designed to exploit this vast new market and keep Japan supplied with goods during the period of hostilities. However, imports of raw materials such as rice, oil and bauxite fell sharply after the first year of the war, and as the Allies began to gain the upper hand, prices of goods began to rise. Having dismantled the local banking structures and replaced them with the Southern Regions Development Bank in April 1942, the new currency rapidly fell in value, and although the State Bank of Burma was set up in 1944, plans for a Burmese currency linked to the yen came too late to be implemented before the tide turned in late 1944 against the Japanese.

Japanese soldiers were expected to play their part in supporting the war effort by taking part in government savings campaigns, and this flimsy document is an example of a Post Office Savings Book, which records deposits of 1 yen, 2 yen, 3 yen, 5 yen, 10 yen, 15 yen and 50 yen. It appears to be spattered with drops of the soldier's blood.

These savings books were frequently found on the bodies of Japanese soldiers, similar in character to British pay-books. One sapper, having found one of these books, and seeing a figure entered in red, exclaimed, 'My God, the little bugger's in debt!'(Quoted in Robert Lyman, *Japan's Last Bid for Victory: The Invasion of India 1944* (Praetorian Press, 2011), p. 186).

To finance the costs of fighting the war the Japanese government mounted intrusive savings campaigns, demanding drastic reductions in consumption and regular savings by the population, including the military.

The government believed that if it could persuade the nation to save large portions of income it would be able to contain wartime inflation and channel savings to finance the war through the Ministry of Finance and the Bank of Japan. The population responded extraordinarily positively, and by 1944 Japanese households were saving approximately 40 per cent of their disposable income.

Savings associations were set up in every neighbourhood, workplace and school. The government took pains to make saving look attractive, reminding people that the money remained theirs, and making interest tax-exempt. At the height of the war in Asia the Japanese were told to sacrifice consumption and save as much as possible to finance the last-ditch 'decisive battle'. By this time in most peoples' minds national saving had become tantamount to national survival.

Dimensions: 22 cm. x 18 cm.

2. BRITISH ARMY WARRANT BOOK

Geoffrey Hayward was another British recruit who served in the Royal Engineers, ending up as a Quartermaster Sergeant when he came home. He was a member of 139 Engineer Stores Regiment, responsible for the equipment needed for bridge and road building and mine clearance. So Geoffrey worked on the management and logistics wing of the Allied Army in Burma, which was in many ways unglamorous, but nevertheless vital, as General Slim was well aware: 'I knew that the campaign in Burma would above all be a supply and transport problem.' (*Defeat Into Victory*, 1956, p. 169).

Geoffrey was called up on 3 April 1941 and reported to Chester Barracks for initial training with the Royal Engineers, designated No. 2148645 Sapper G. Hayward, RE. He was paid 10s per week, and given his 'Soldier's Service and Pay Book, Army Book 64', covered in brown canvas, which instructed the soldier to 'always carry this book on your person'.

Very soon Geoffrey was promoted to Lance Corporal and posted to C. E. Northern Command at York. On 10 November 1941 he embarked on the SS *Narkunda* (P&O Line) for an unknown destination, but issued with tropical kit. The rumour was that they were headed for India. After a stop for refuelling and fresh supplies at Freetown, Sierra Léone, where they were not allowed off the troopship, the convoy was escorted by destroyers and later by the battleship HMS *Royal Sovereign* to Durban where they were given shore leave. They changed troopships to the *Capetown Castle* (Union Castle Line), and were promoted from sleeping on the floor to the comparative luxury of bunk beds. On 10 January 1942 they arrived at Bombay and were transferred to the Royal Bombay Sappers and Miners at Kirkee, a town and army base near Poona. There they were held in a 'pool' for movement to the Field Service Area as required. In April Geoffrey was posted to 110 Company Royal Engineers Works in north-east Assam and promoted to Corporal, five months later becoming a Staff Sergeant. After nearly three years at the base, during which time he had worked on the construction of the Dimapur–Imphal road and become a Warrant Officer, Geoffrey was sent to the Homeward Bound Troop Depot, Deolali, which was a British Army transit camp about 100 miles north-east of Bombay. The soldiers' nickname for the camp, 'Doolally' became a slang term associated with mental illness because soldiers often had to wait long periods in the camp for a troopship back home, and sometimes broke down because of the heat, boredom and disease. He eventually embarked on a troopship for his repatriation back to England, where he arrived on 15 July 1945, to be greeted by his mother Ellen, who had been waiting anxiously for his return. His well-worn Service and Pay Book, which he had successfully kept safe during his years in Burma, holds his record of employment, his promotions, his awards, which include being mentioned in dispatches, his inoculations against typhus and cholera, and perhaps most importantly his army pay, which began at 10s but gradually rose as he gained in rank and seniority. This small book, no doubt kept in his breast pocket, is a detailed record of Geoffrey Hayward's service in the Burma Campaign and the part he played in the Allies' eventual victory over the Japanese.

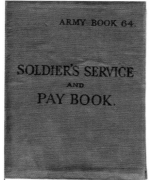

3. JAPANESE FAMILY PHOTOGRAPHS

These photographs, which form part of John Alexander's collection, may have come from a single Japanese soldier, or from several.

The family group shows the soldier's sister Kïmiko, and his two brothers Ikuhiko and Kenzo, and are dated December 1942.

The picture of the girl standing in the open boat bears the caption on the back 'In a swim suit', perhaps a girlfriend or wife back home.

The stately young lady standing on a small log bridge is a Burmese lady from the Shan States in traditional costume worn for formal celebrations.

It is impossible to know who these individuals were, but these personal photographs, which so many soldiers carried with them, are a reminder that on both sides of the conflict were young men far from home, who longed to return to their loved ones one day.

Dimensions:
Family Photograph: 10.5 cm x 7.5 cm
Girl in Swim Suit: 7 cm x 9.5 cm
Girl in Burmese Costume: 6 cm x 9 cm

Chapter II

From Reigate to Ranchi

John Willis Alexander was born in 1921, one of four children. He grew up in Reigate, Surrey, and at the age of seven he was enrolled in the Choir School of King's College, Cambridge, going on from there to his father's old school, Ardingly College, in Sussex. Along with most of his contemporaries he joined the School Officers Training Corps, and on the outbreak of the Second World War he enlisted and joined the Royal Engineers. He was sent for training to Albuhera Barracks at the Aldershot Garrison in Surrey where he spent six months learning to be a sapper, and ended up training ATS girls to drive, even though at that stage he could himself only ride a motorbike! At one of the regular Aldershot dances he was paired with a young Audrey Harker for the Paul Jones, and after that they began seeing each other. However, soon afterwards John was given his posting, as a Lieutenant in 63 Brigade, part of the 17th Indian Division. The division was formed on 1 June 1941 with Divisional Headquarters at Ahmednagar, about 70 miles

Officer Training Corps, Ardingly College, Sussex, 1939. (Author's collection)

north-east of Poona, and later moved to Dhond, a city in the state of Maharashtra, on the margins of the Deccan plateau. There were two military camps there, where the division was trained in desert warfare. However, they were then sent to Moulmein in Burma in January 1942 and formed the Tenasserim Command, together with 16th Indian Infantry Brigade, tasked with stopping the Japanese advance up the Tenasserim coast. John sailed from England in a troop ship on the long voyage to India, where the ship docked at Bombay. He then travelled by train across India for three days and nights in sultry heat to Ranchi where there was a large training camp. After a couple of months there he boarded another train, which took him to Calcutta. The Movement Officer sent him over the Hooghly River on the splendid Howrah Bridge to the Grand Hotel, Chowringhee. Most junior officers who were to serve in Burma must have stayed there. I have stayed in recent years in its air-conditioned splendour, but in those days it was a Turkish bath, the air barely stirred by the fans and punkahs. The only respite was to be found in the hotel bar where iced drinks temporarily cooled the body and slaked the thirst.

After sailing by sea from Calcutta to Rangoon, John joined his division, which soon went into action against the 33rd and 35th Divisions of the Japanese 15th Army. It must have been a considerable shock for those young and inexperienced soldiers, who had arrived in Burma fresh and innocent, suddenly to have to come to terms with a ruthless enemy using jungle warfare tactics in the tropical surroundings of Burma. What was this strange and exotic country in which John Alexander now found himself, and why was he part of an army fighting to save it from being overrun by the Japanese Empire?

Above left: Audrey Harker, aged eighteen. (Author's collection)

Above right: Scene at Mao on the Dimapur–Kohima road showing a convoy of trucks carrying men of the Royal Engineers to Imphal, January 1942. Geoffrey Hayward worked on this section of road in north-eastern India. (© Imperial War Museum)

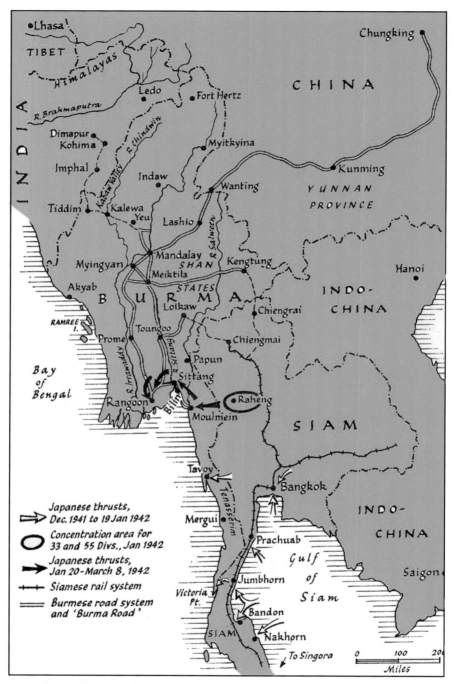

BURMA

Map showing the routes taken by the Allied Armies in the retreat from Burma, 1942. (Burma Star Association)

Burma lies to the east of the Bay of Bengal, a country bounded on the north and east by China, on the north-west by Bengal and Assam, and on the west and south-west by the sea. It is shaped like a hand, with a long forefinger pointing south. The hand divides into fingers, mountain ranges stretching southwards. Between them are the valleys of the three chief rivers, the Chindwin, the Irrawaddy and the Salween. The long forefinger is the coastal strip known as Tenasserim. The mountain ranges form barriers on the west towards the Arakan and India, and in the north-east with China. The Irrawaddy runs down through the elongated central plain, and is navigable by steamer from the delta for 900 miles to Bhamo in the north.

The rainy season starts with the south-westerly monsoon winds in May and continues until October, making the roads and tracks impassible and causing havoc for an army on the move. In the nineteenth and early twentieth century railways were built from south of Moulmein to as far north as Myitkyina, serving Rangoon, Mandalay, Toungoo and Prome, and these became vital lines of communication for both sides in the conflict.

The Bamars, descended from Indo-Tibetan nomads who conquered the central plains in the ninth and tenth centuries AD, comprise about 70 per cent of the population, but there is also a complex jigsaw of minority peoples such as the Rakhines, Shan and Karen who live in the border areas. Buddhism, the main religion, took root in the fifth century BC, and Burma has more stupas, or pagodas, than any other country. Often gilded, their tapering spires dominate the skyline, complemented by the thousands of red-robed monks who fill the village streets at festival time.

Burma has vast teak forests, and is rich in minerals, especially tin, coal, oil, gas, rubies, sapphires and other precious stones. In the plains large amounts of sugarcane and rice grow. In the early seventeenth century the English East India Company established factories in Burma, and British merchants were already settling in the country. Relations were often tense between the Burmese and the British, and matters came to a head when the Burmese General Maha Bandula, planning to take control of the Arakan, invaded Manipur. The British Government declared war on Burma in 1824, and after successive Anglo-Burmese wars Burma became a Province of British India in 1886.

The whole country became a major province of the British Empire under a Lieutenant-Governor in 1897, the monarchy was abolished, and a secular education system introduced, which discouraged Buddhism and traditional Burmese culture. This caused growing resentment and sowed the seeds of political resistance that later grew into open insurgency and collaboration when the Japanese invaded.

A peaceful scene before the campaign in Burma engulfed this border area. The Naga Bazaar at Imphal in January 1942. (© Imperial War Museum)

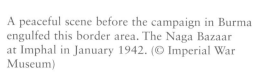

17

Objects: 4. Official History of 17th Div., 5. Johns Army Kit.

4. HISTORY OF 17 INDIAN DIVISION

This history of the 17th Indian Division, July 1941 to December 1945, was published in India and printed by G. A. Lyons at Thacker's Press and Directories Ltd, Bentinck Street, Calcutta. It has sand-coloured covers with the famous 'Black Cat' insignia on the front. There is an accompanying slipcase with twelve maps illustrating the campaign and a large folding map of India, Ceylon and Burma.

The book gives a detailed account of the Burma campaign, and explains in the introduction:

1. THIS history is a narrative of the life of 17 Ind Div from its formation in July 1941 in India to the completion of its task in re-establishing, by 31 December, 1945, the British Administration in the TENASSERIM Civil Division in BURMA.

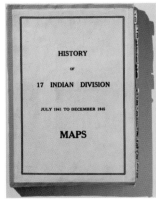

2. As it is a narrative account of operations, tactical lessons and reports on campaigns are not included. Complete records do not exist of the Order of Battle, details of casualties, etc., during the first Burma Campaigns in 1942 and some of the information has been obtained from the personal recollections of officers who have served almost continuously with the Division since its formation.

   The history has been compiled within the Division and is not an 'Official History'.

3. The Division was in action against the Japanese in Burma and Assam, with a few short breaks for reorganisation and training from January 1942, until the Japanese surrender in August 1945, and has fought against the Japanese longer than any other British or Indian formation.
4. The following units have been under command of 17 Ind Div during its whole period of Active Service:-

60 Ind Fd Coy	59 Ind Ord Mob Wksp Coy
17 Ind Div Sigs	37 Ind Fd Amb
4/12 FFR	22 Ind Fd Hyg Sec
7/10 BALUCH	17 Ind Div Fd Security Service Section
1/7 GR	

The book is divided into thirteen parts, which trace the fortunes of the division from their first encounters with the advancing Japanese forces in the area around Tavoy in January 1942, to the surrender of the Japanese in August 1945 and the division's reoccupation of Tenasserim. The process of disarming Japanese forces, collecting arms, guarding supply dumps, and establishing a British Military Administration in the area took until December 1945. Huge amounts of equipment were collected, including 50,000 Japanese rifles, 9,917 swords and over 3,000 tons of ammunition. The account states that 'The civil population was very glad to see British troops back in the district. Although many of them had collaborated with the Japanese, they had discovered that British rule was greatly preferable.' On 1 January 1946 the Military Administration handed over the Tenasserim area to the Governor of Burma and the civil authorities.

During the campaign seven Victoria Crosses, twenty-seven Distinguished Service Orders, 184 Military Crosses and 276 Military Medals were awarded to soldiers serving in units within the 17th Indian Division. The history concludes:

1. 17 Indian Division fought throughout the 1942 campaign at a great disadvantage. They were untrained in the type of fighting which they met and were an uncohesive miscellany of units which had never previously worked together. Furthermore the Japanese had the initiative and it was not possible to have sufficient breathing space to get the force properly organised.
2. During 1943 and 1944 conditions were more equal and, except for their abortive advance to IMPHAL and KOHIMA, the Japanese did not succeed in increasing their gains and the initiative gradually passed to us.
3. Finally in 1945, the Division as a well-equipped, trained and co-ordinated formation made their victorious advance back through Burma and reoccupied the area from which they had withdrawn in 1942. In Oct 1945, Div HQ was established in MOULMEIN where it had been in Jan 1942.
4. The record of the "BLACK CAT" Division had been unequalled by any other formation in the Burma theatre. The Division was twice reported by the Japanese to have been annihilated but, in spite of this, was largely responsible for the victorious conclusion of the campaign.

Dimensions:
History: 24 cm x 18.5 cm
Map Folder: 24 cm x 16.5 cm

5. JOHN ALEXANDER'S UNIFORM, EQUIPMENT, AND INSIGNIA

John Alexander retained much of his own uniform and equipment at the end of the campaign and brought it back to England. His army tunic does not seem particularly suitable for jungle warfare, but that is because when the division was first formed in July 1941 at Ahmednagar in India, and then moved to Dhond in November for training, the expectation was that it would be deployed to the Middle East. The division's vehicles were still painted in the 'Yellow Stone' colour appropriate to the Middle East, and the men were still wearing their khaki shorts, shirts and jackets.

The badges and insignia John wore included the grenade lapel badge, showing a brass grenade that had been adopted in 1825 by the Sappers and Miners, with the RE motto 'Ubique' on a scroll underneath, meaning 'everywhere' and reflecting the fact that the corps had been involved in nearly all the British Army's combat deployments.

There are also shoulder tabs with the Crown and 'R. E.', the badge of S.E.A.C. (South-East Asia Command), the XIVth Army, and the badge of the 19th Indian Infantry Division – a yellow dagger held in a clenched hand on a red background. (For the badge of the 17th Indian Division, see object no. 12). John also brought back one of his sappers' tools in a neat leather holster, and reinforced knee-pads suitable for those involved in mine clearance. He also brought back his tiny bivouac tent, which must have offered scant protection against the monsoon rains. All these items were packed in his heavy steel army trunk, inscribed with his name, rank and number, 214864 CAPT J.W. ALEXANDER RE, his address 11 Castlefield Road, Reigate, Surrey, and marked 'Not Wanted on Voyage'.

John was also awarded four medals for his service in Burma: the 1939–45 Burma Campaign Medal with a ribbon of dark blue, red and light blue in three equal vertical stripes; the Burma Star with the Royal and Imperial cypher surmounted by a crown and surrounded by a circlet containing the words 'The Burma Star', with a red ribbon edged with dark blue and orange; the Defense Medal; and the War Medal 1939–45 with the ribbon showing a narrow central red stripe with a narrow white stripe at either edge and two intervening strips in blue.

Chapter III

An Army in Retreat

As well as being rich in natural resources, Burma also formed a strategic barrier between the rest of South-East Asia, China and India. If Burma was captured by an invading army, it would be able to threaten the eastern flank of the British Empire, and to attack China and cut her supply lines from the south. This was Burma's military significance, and the reason there was a Burma Campaign.

Lieutenant-Colonel Frank Owen, in his account of the campaign published by HMSO in 1946, describes the Japanese advance:

> Japan's surge of conquest, piling up from Pearl Harbour to Singapore, swept the Americans, British and Dutch from their holdings in the South-West Pacific in little more than a hundred days of cataclysm. Within a week of Pearl Harbour the Japanese had burst into Burma, too, for Burma forms the natural strategic shield of these conquests. The Himalayas seal off the north; the mountains which extend down the length of Burma form successive ramparts against assault from the west. Once conquered, the Japanese High Command reckoned that the only way that attack could come upon this Burma 'barrier land' was from the south through the port of Rangoon.
>
> The Japanese poured in across the south-eastern frontiers from Siam. Overwhelming resistance, or rushing round it as a tide floods up between the sandbanks, they reached the head of the Burmese River valleys under the northern arc of mountains, and there they established their front.

The 17th Indian Division held Mergui, Tavoy and Moulmein, but as the Japanese forces in superior numbers advanced on Tavoy, they fell back, shocked and demoralised by the swiftness and ferocity of the Japanese advance. As described by Lieutenant-Colonel Frank Owen, this was an army in retreat:-

> Red eyes, grey faces, beards, their shirts torn with jungle thorns, striped black with tonight's wet sweat and white with yesterday's dried salt of sweat. Water bottles rattle from their belts, as dry as their own lips. Many an ammunition pouch is empty too, for these troops have come out of four day's battle. Dirt and blood stain the rags that bind their wounds. They have been marching with short halts for the past 24 hours, and there has been no time to wash, even if there was water. These soldiers are marching towards another battle.

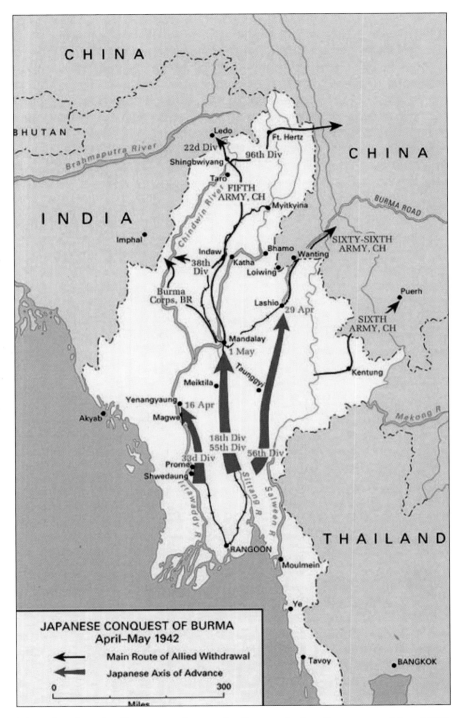

Map showing the Japanese advance in Burma during January to May 1942. (Wikipedia Commons)

For twenty-two days the 17th Division had been withdrawing, bombed and machine-gunned from the air, and constantly frustrated by the standard Japanese tactic of throwing a roadblock across the path of retreat, covered by machine-gun fire. The division had been ordered to retire beyond the Sittang River, the last watery line of defence between the Japanese forces and Rangoon.

There was fierce fighting in the dense jungle around Mokpalin Bridge over the Sittang River. When Brigadier Hugh Jones MC, officer commanding the bridge, could not hold out any longer, the decision was taken to blow up the bridge to stop the Japanese pouring across it. On 23 February 1942 the sappers blew the bridge with two brigades of the 17th Indian Division still on the enemy side. John Alexander recalled that 'All units suffered heavily. Our force was badly disorganised'. The day after the battle the 17th Indian Division numbered 3,350 men and 149 officers. But the shattered units lived to fight another day. They regrouped at Pegu, were joined by 63 Indian Infantry Brigade, and withdrew towards Prome. The division was by now led by Major-General David Cowan, and the Corps HQ was set up at Prome under Lieutenant-General Bill Slim. 'Burcorps' now consisted of the 17th Indian Division, four Battalions of the Burma Rifles, 7 Armoured Brigade and a handful of aircraft operating from India.

During the withdrawal to and beyond Prome the Allies were attacked not just by the Japanese forces, but by units of the Burma Independence Army. This was formed from a group known as 'The Thirty Comrades', including Aung San, who was working for Burmese independence. Their slogan was 'Colonialism's difficulty is freedom's opportunity', and they held rallies with cries such as 'May the British be bombed and defeated!' In 1938 Aung San had joined the radical, anti-colonial party known as the 'Thakins', who combined with others to form the Freedom Block. They opposed co-operating with the British unless they were guaranteed independence immediately after the war ended. The British refused to co-operate and imprisoned most of the leadership. Aung San, a former student at Rangoon University and a charismatic but difficult character, at first sought help from the Chinese to form an independent Burmese Army, but was contacted by a Japanese Colonel Keiji Suzuki and recruited to form a resistance army to work with Japan against the British.

To understand the feelings of the Burmese people at the outbreak of the campaign, you have only to read George Orwell's novel *Burmese Days*, published in 1934. Orwell spent five years from 1922 to 1927 as a police officer in the Indian Imperial Police Force in Burma, and his novel is a savage critique of British Imperialism and its corrosive effect on individuals and cultures. Set in the fictional district of Kyauktada in Upper Burma, it tells the story of John Flory, a thirty-five-year-old timber merchant, who has spent all his adult life in Burma. The novel criticises the inherent racism of the British whom Orwell believed used their Imperial presence as a pretence to rob and exploit the native people. It helps us to understand why the Burmese resented British rule and at first welcomed the Japanese, and why the Burmese Independence Army collaborated with the Japanese. The BIA was officially formed in December 1941 with Colonel Suzuki as Commander in Chief, and Aung San as Senior Staff Officer. However, it soon became clear to the Burmese that they were in reality stooges of the Japanese, who treated them harshly and ignored their requests to form local governments of their own. The Burmese soon discovered that they had exchanged a relatively benign imperial power for a much more aggressive and brutal version, and eventually, after discussions with the British High Command in 1944, the BIA revolted against the Japanese in March 1945. Lord

Japanese forces enter Tavoy in Tennasserim, cheered on by the Burmese, 1942. (© Imperial War Museum)

Aerial reconnaissance photograph of the bridge over the Sittang River, destroyed on the retreat northwards in the face of advancing Japanese forces on 23 February 1942. (© Imperial War Museum)

Louis Mountbatten formally recognised them as an ally and armed them to help push the Japanese south.

During the British retreat, however, sensing that they had a real chance of pushing the British out of Burma, the 'Thakins', numbering about 4,000, were a fanatical foe, and especially aggressive towards the Indian Divisions because they detested the many thousands of Indians brought in by the British administration in Burma as labourers on the railways and other public works, and who had also cornered lucrative sections of the economy. Harassed on all sides by the Japanese advance and by Burmese patriot forces, and with much looting and burning of villages and oilfields, 'the land of a million pagodas burned'.

This Burmese National Army had its counterpart in India too, where Subhas Chandra Bose, a radical member of the Indian National Congress was a defiant nationalist, and totally opposed to India entering the war on the Allies' side. After Pearl Harbour, at a conference of Axis powers about India, Bose called for a tripartite declaration by Germany, Russia and Japan, but Hitler remained unconvinced, and Bose realised that he had to deal directly with Japan. The surrender of Malaya and Singapore led to the formation of the Indian National Army, composed of some of those who had surrendered to the Japanese.

olonel Aung San
d Daw Khin Kyi
:er their marriage
September 1942.
'ikimedia Commons)

Although the INA was the military wing of the Indian Independence League, the Japanese Imperial General Headquarters was reluctant to give them independent command, and in any case looked down on the fighting abilities of Indians, seeing them mainly as a propaganda tool. Nevertheless, Subhas Chandra Bose recruited widely for the INA in Malaya, and was confident that 'when I land in Bengal everyone will revolt. Wavell's whole army will join me'. He announced the formation of the Provisional Government of Free India and declared himself head of state. His pretentions to independence were indulged by the Japanese military command, even though they had no interest in Indian independence.

By late 1943 Bose had raised a second INA and assembled a force of 40,000 men and women. In May 1944 Bose's brigade was sent to Kohima and managed to plant an Indian flag in the town, but in subsequent offensives the INA suffered heavy losses. Of 9,000 INA soldiers deployed in 1944 about 1,000 were killed or wounded, between 2,000 and 3,000 died of disease or starvation, and about 700 officers and men surrendered. Bose was regarded as a political threat by the British, but as a fighting force the INA was no match for the Indian Army.

The sheer numbers of the Japanese 15th Army, reinforced by five additional divisions, made a further Allied withdrawal towards Mandalay necessary. There were heavy casualties on both sides, but magnificent engineering work by the sappers of 63 Brigade, and good staff planning, created a line of supply routes fit for motor transport, so the army could march in good order.

By March 1942 the 17th Indian Division was on the Tiddim Road, the sappers blowing the bridges behind them, and building the road through to the Manipur River, in spite of heavy rain and mud. In order to protect the Chinese 5th Army the whole of the 17th Indian Division was withdrawn to Meiktila, with 63 Brigade securing the Ava Bridge at Sagaing on the Irrawaddy River and then given covering support while they were ferried across. The troops fought a brilliant rearguard action at Kyaukse, south of Mandalay, to cover the passage of their armour over the Ava Bridge, and then at dawn on 30 April 1942 British sappers, including John Alexander, blew two spans of the bridge, a major factor in slowing the advance of the Japanese. After a fierce rearguard action at the ferry at Kalewa, the Japanese were repulsed. The British burned their tanks and stores, and crossed the Chindwin River. The day after they crossed, the monsoon rains broke as the troops marched 100 miles on foot to Tamu. By the untiring efforts of the engineers it had been possible to move the whole of the 17th Indian Division safely to Tamu. Although the Japanese had suffered many casualties and some prisoners had been taken, by now the Allied forces were very tired and short of food and water. Lieutenant-Colonel Frank Owen described their retreat through the jungle:

> Soldiers stumbled onward weakened by wounds and privation, until they dropped or a comrade held them up. Indians threw away their dilapidated boots and plodded on with raw feet. Uniforms were rags, and equipment had long since been shed: one thing all held on to – their weapons. Some British battalions were reduced to 100 men. This army in retreat also carried with them along their trackless route 2,000 sick and wounded, whom they refused to abandon to the mercies of the enemy.

A Chinese girl from one of the Japanese Army's 'Comfort Battalions' awaits interrogation at a camp in Rangoon.

Young women from Korea, China, the Philippines and Burma were lured with promises of factory or nursing jobs to work as prostitutes for the Japanese military machine. It is estimated that around 200,000 women were recruited to serve in military brothels, of whom approximately three quarters died. They were taken from Asian countries occupied by the Japanese and moved around the theatres of war as the Japanese advanced.

Before the launch of *Operation C* against Imphal and Kohima in 1944, the Japanese Commander of the 15th Army, General Mutaguchi, was so confident of success that he ordered the entire complement of the 15th Army's comfort women to be moved to Imphal so that his men could be instantly rewarded for their efforts once Imphal had been taken. (© Imperial War Museum)

General Bill Slim, however, commented at the time: 'They might look like scarecrows, but they looked like soldiers too.'

At last, the retreat had come to an end, and the Burma Army had marched into India. A distance of 1,100 miles had been covered by the 17th Indian Division from Moulmein to Imphal in five months. General Alexander's army was incorporated into the IV Corps of the Indian Command based at Imphal. Meanwhile General Stilwell, with the remnants of V Chinese Army, fell back to Shwebo in the north. While the

Subhas Chandra Bose surrounded by members of the Indian National Army. (Wikimedia Commons)

Above and below: The Ava Bridge over the Irrawaddy. (From an album owned by George Feasey, 2nd British Division: Chris Pearce)

Burmese refugees flee along the Prome Road into India, during the Allied retreat, January 1942. (© Imperial War Museum)

Chinese eventually retreated through the Hukawng Valley into China, General Stilwell was forced by the rapid Japanese advance on Myitkyina to strike out west through the hills to Imphal. The Allied forces had disappeared over the mountains into India and China, and all the land of Burma passed to Japan.

Objects: 6. Lettercard and Postcard, 7. Burmese Knife, 8. Jap Colour Sketches.

6. JAPANESE LETTERCARDS AND POSTCARDS

Among the objects John retrieved from Japanese soldiers are two military service lettercards and two postcards. One of the postcards is very faded and tattered, but the other shows an attractive street scene in China, with vendors, street traders and rickshaw drivers all in brightly painted clothes. It was originally drawn by Kojima Matsunosuke.

On the back of one of the lettercards are what appear to be notes about the locations and names of various army units, partly in Assam and partly in the Arakan. These notes probably relate to the movement northwards of Japanese troops as they invaded Burma in 1942.

Dimensions:
Lettercard: 13.5 cm. x 9 cm.
Postcard: 14 cm. x 9 cm.

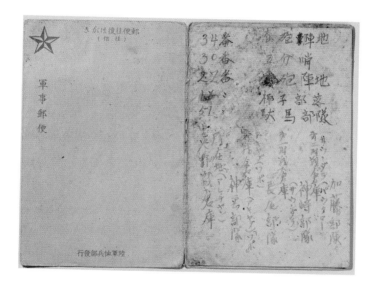

7. BURMESE KNIFE

This fine silver-mounted knife from the Shan people in the Eastern States of Burma is one of the finest objects that John Alexander brought back from the Burma Campaign. It is a *dha hmyaung*, a Burmese term meaning 'blade', 24 cm in length, and decorated with applied silver wire work. The hilt is encased in fine wound wire, and it has a single-edged steel blade with a sharp point. The hilt and scabbard fit together so smoothly that the seam is practically invisible. It consists of an inner core of timber that is covered in chased silver sheet, decorated with inlaid silver thread. The metal has been hammered onto a prepared surface and annealed by heating. The flared base is typical of the region.

These small knives had a multitude of uses, one of which was to slice up betel nuts to make a substance that was chewed as a mild narcotic. However, the quality of this piece suggests that it may have been reserved for ceremonial use or as a status symbol for officials. The usual means of wearing the *dha hmyaung* was by a cord baldric, slung over the shoulder or suspended from a waist belt.

The origins of this particular knife are unclear, but John Alexander always maintained that it originally came from a Burmese 'comfort woman'. Comfort women were girls from various parts of South-East Asia, including Indonesia, Malaya, Siam and Burma, who were recruited by the Imperial Japanese Army, under compulsion, to be sex slaves during the Second World War in one of the largest systems of sexual violence and trafficking in modern history. About 200,000 girls and women in Asia are believed to have been forced to work in military brothels, in a system approved and set up by the Emperor of Japan himself. After the war the Japanese government denied that such a system ever existed, and to this day no official acknowledgement or apology has ever been given. Perhaps this beautiful knife did once belong to an unknown 'comfort girl', a fine piece of Burmese craft and a means of protection against the brutality of the Japanese military machine.

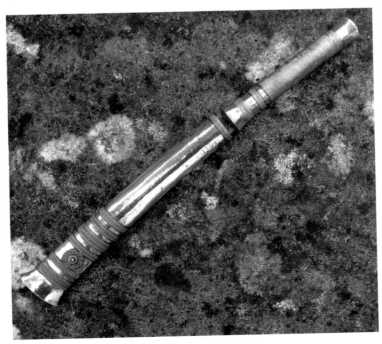

8. JAPANESE COLOURED SKETCHES

One of the most attractive objects in John Alexander's collection is a folder of coloured sketches that must have been made by a Japanese soldier (possibly Shoichi Yoshida), during a period when he was not in the combat zone. The sketches, dated between May 1942 and February 1943, are drawn in pen, pencil and watercolour on small pieces of drawing paper, which have then been stuck, in groups of two and four, onto larger pages that have become yellow with age.

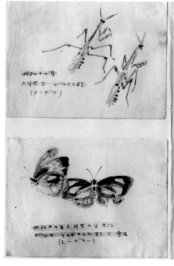
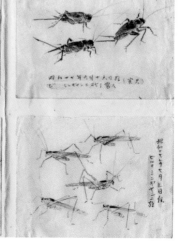

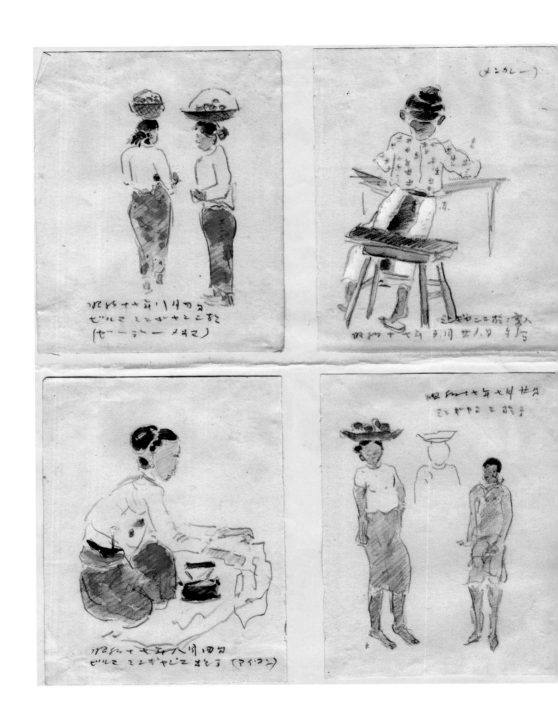

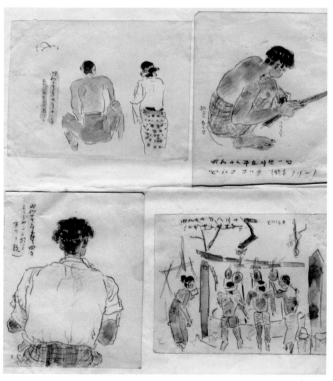

The subject matter includes scenes from village life, birds, insects, and plants, all drawn with a delicate but deft hand. These scenes were sketched during the period when Japanese forces controlled the whole of central Burma as well as the northern frontier region.

Ordinary Burmese villagers must have watched in amazement as Japanese soldiers and Burmese fighters marched side by side through their towns and villages, established their headquarters, and set up military camps in strategic locations across the country. Second Lieutenant Shoichi Yoshida would have been one of these soldiers, equally curious to see and understand the land his forces had so rapidly occupied. There are thirty-eight sketches in total, many clearly drawn in the area around Yenangyaung and Myingyan. One of the Japanese objectives had been to capture the oilfields around Yenangyaung, although the Allies destroyed most of the wells and demolished the refinery as they retreated. Myingyan was a city on the east bank of the Irrawaddy River to the south of Mandalay, and part of the Meiktila Division of Upper Burma.

It was also the terminus of a branch railway to Thazi and on the main railway line between Yangon and Mandalay. Both places were of considerable strategic importance, where Japanese troops would have been stationed during the occupation.

If Shoichi Yoshida was the artist, he clearly took delight in recording local people at work, including one captioned '*Chef Sori*', and dated 31 May 1842, another showing a group of Burmese standing around a well drawing water, captioned '*Myingyan, Burma*' and dated 10 August, and pen and wash drawings of a pagoda and 'a restaurant', dated 21 and 22 December 1942. The drawings of the pagoda and the restaurant are particularly appealing.

Every village seemed to have its own pagoda, with perhaps a monastery nearby. The pagodas of Burma have a very satisfying form, bell-shaped, tapering in concave fashion to a high narrow finial from which hung bells that tinkled in the breeze. The larger pagodas, such as those at Pagan, Rangoon and Mandalay, often enclosed a figure of the Buddha, perhaps gold-plated, gazing out impassively over the chaos of the conflict. The spire too might be gold-plated, which would glint enticingly in the evening sun.

There are also drawings of 'Foreign Dolls', dated August 1942, and four beautiful drawings of local birds made in Myingyan in July 1942, and captioned 'Sir-Bird', 'Chi in a little hatch', and 'Sarnie', possibly nicknames given to pet birds.

The artist had acute powers of observation and gave his sketches a great sense of liveliness and humanity. It is puzzling and disconcerting to reflect that the same soldier who could produce these lovely sketches was also capable of using Allied prisoners, tied to trees, as bayonet practice and subjecting them to other brutal and sadistic forms of torture. This was one of the paradoxes of the Japanese spirit and character which the Allies found difficult to comprehend or to forgive.

Coloured Sketches:

   a) Sketches of dolls and lady, 18 December 1942.
   b) Lizard on a branch, November 1942.
   c) Grasshoppers, crickets, and butterfly, Myingyan, 1942.
   d) Girl ironing, Myingyan, August 1942.
   e) Girl weighing fruit, Myingyan, August 1942.
   f) Restaurant and pagoda, Myingylin, 21 and 22 December 1942.
   g) Two sketches of coconut tree, Yenangyaung, 17 February 1943.
   h) Flowers, Yenangyaung, November 1942.
   i) People at a well.

Dimensions:
14.5 cm x 9 cm.
11 cm x 9 cm.

Chapter IV

Getting the Measure of the Enemy

When the 17th Indian Division arrived at Imphal a line of communications was established to Kohima and the railhead at Dimapur. By November 1942 the division had moved into training camps, and set about regaining their strength in the Chin Hills. The Allied forces had been comprehensively defeated and had lost 13,000 men. The army had lost cohesion and a lot of its equipment. It had also lost confidence in its own ability and in its leadership. But the Allied forces had not been knocked out, and most importantly they had learnt some important lessons the hard way about their formidable enemy. General Bill Slim summed up the forces they were up against:

> The strength of the Japanese Army lay, not in its higher leadership, which, once its career of success had been checked, became confused, nor in its special aptitude for jungle warfare, but in the spirit of the individual Japanese soldier. He fought and marched till he died. If 500 Japanese were ordered to hold a position, we had to kill 495 before it was ours – and then the last five killed themselves. It was this combination of obedience and ferocity that made the Japanese Army, whatever its condition, so formidable, and which would make any army formidable.
>
> Field Marshall Viscount Slim, *Defeat into Victory*
> (Pan Books, 2009), p. 615

What, then, were the influences that had moulded these people into such a powerful military machine, and why was the Japanese army advancing so swiftly into South-East Asia? Until what is known as the Meiji period Japan exercised little influence on the world stage except as part of the complex of trade routes that included much of South-East Asia. The Meiji era extended from 1868 to 1912, and during this period Japan evolved from an isolated feudal society into an industrial nation state, influenced by western ideas and technology. After the overthrow of the Shogunate in 1868 the ruling military cliques restored an imperial system of government which established the Emperor as the Godhead central to the constitutional and spiritual life of the nation, with Shintoism as the State Religion. The Red Sun disc and the Rising Sun Ensign of the Imperial Japanese Navy became major symbols in the emerging Japanese Empire.

The ancient Samurai Warrior culture, based on Bushidō, the legendary way of the warrior, had evolved from ideals based on medieval warfare to ideals of service, honour and the pursuit of the arts by the nineteenth century, but after the 'Satsuma Rebellion' of 1877, when its defeated leader Saigo Takamori retreated to a cave to perform ritual suicide, the Samurai class died out. However, the Samurai ideal remained within Japanese consciousness, and this now re-emerged, combined with a Darwinian belief in Japan's destiny to dominate Asia, and a conviction of its superiority to western nations.

During the 1930s the rise of militarism, and conflicts with both Russia and China, emboldened the army to recruit from the rural peasantry and mould them into an Imperial Army disciplined by violence and brutal tests of endurance to serve the nation at the pleasure of the Emperor.

'Fear, anger and a desire for revenge on the battlefield existed alongside the brutality meeted out to new recruits as a necessary "baptism of blood"' (Christopher Harding, *Japan Story* (Penguin, 2019). This led to a growing reputation for brutality, culminating in the Massacre of Nanking in December 1937, when General Matsui Iwane rode into the city on horseback at the head of his troops and presided over widespread atrocities.

This aggression was based on the coming together of the old militarist tradition, political nationalism, and a belief that the Japanese were superior to western cultural norms, which grew out of a Zen Buddhist understanding that reality is ultimately 'nothingness', and that in Japan the Buddha's teachings had reached their highest realisation. The state was a divinely revealed identity animated by the will of the Emperor, and the individual's profoundest moment of self-realisation came when he merged himself with the will of the Emperor.

A Japanese family holding a Good Luck Flag. (Wikipedia Commons)

In 1937 the government published a document 'Fundamentals of Our National Polity', which set out the rejection of Western Enlightenment thought, and emphasised the need for the nation to ground itself on the Japanese spirit focused on the Emperor. In the summer of 1940 the government announced the creation of a 'Greater East Asia Co-Prosperity Sphere', which was in reality a smokescreen for Japanese imperialism and expansion. When in December 1941 the United States of America tried to counter Japanese aggression in South-East Asia by insisting that Japan withdraw its troops from China, Japan, sensing that conflict was inevitable, struck first and bombed Pearl Harbour.

This was the situation in Japan, and their accompanying outlook on the rest of the world, when Shoichi Yoshida joined the army. He had joined an organisation with an intensely hierarchical structure within an officer corps who lacked imagination, and who were over-optimistic about success when engaging the enemy. They were easily confused by the unexpected, slow to adjust, and reluctant to change a plan, because they feared losing face by admitting mistakes and failures. The Japanese used the tactic of 'the hook' during the Burma Campaign, which involved carrying out a holding action in the front against Allied oncoming forces, while moving a mobile force in a wide arc around the flank and attacking from the rear. At first this tactic was very successful, but once the Allies understood it and learned to fight back, the Japanese became confused, and often either squandered their strength in useless banzai charges, or defended positions to the last man when a tactical retreat would have served them better. Japanese positions were usually solidly constructed, with troops well dug in. Although Japanese soldiers were tenacious, cunning and courageous, their tactics were basically defensive, bolstered by a nihilistic culture of each soldier not caring whether he lived or died. 'Death before surrender' was a genuinely held belief and not just a propaganda slogan.

As Patrick Davis remarks in his memoir *A Child At Arms* (London 1970):

> We knew that the Japanese soldier was taught to prefer death to surrender. Death was a victory of the spiritual over the material. A man's honour was everything and surrender was the ultimate dishonour: a prisoner would have no rights, could never, so he was told, return to Japan. This was no theory, acknowledged on the barrack square, ignored in the field. Up to December 1944 the number of prisoners taken was so few that for an Allied soldier to have seen one was an 'occasion'. Not for us the luxury of capturing hundreds of our enemy. In two campaigns my battalion had not taken one.

Such was their contempt for surrender, the Japanese held those they themselves took prisoner in deep contempt. Their own sense of racial and cultural superiority meant that they despised other races, and the brutal regime under which they had been trained meant that they treated prisoners harshly and sadistically. They had a similar callous disregard for the sick and the injured, ignoring them for as long as possible, and providing only a rudimentary medical system, with the result that thousands died who could have been saved. The Japanese High Command in Burma eventually learned the hard and bitter way that willpower, discipline and the human spirit alone could not conquer all obstacles.

However, as the Japanese Army poured in across the south-eastern frontiers of Siam in January 1942, overwhelming resistance, and pushing the Allies back inexorably to the head of the river valleys under the northern arc of mountains that separated Burma from India and China, their philosophy and tactics appeared to make them invincible. Allied troops, outmanned and poorly trained, were quickly demoralised, and further weakened by malaria, dysentery and typhus. They were not completely broken, but they had learnt some hard lessons. It was time for the Allied forces to reorganise, rethink their strategy and regain their fighting spirit.

During the remainder of 1942 the 17th Indian Division was in training camps in the Chin Hills, with three battalions at Ranchi, capital of the state of Jharkhand, India. During this period John Alexander, along with other officers, was granted a period of leave and returned to England. His diary for the last months of 1942 shows that he was based at Aldershot Barracks, but also able to see his sweetheart, Audrey Harker. He had clearly fallen head over heels in love with her, as the many expressions of love and devotion in his diary attest. She had joined the WRNS, and was eventually posted to HMS Collingwood at Portsmouth doing administrative work, ending up in London based at Queen Anne's Mansions towards the end of the war. On 16 December 1942 John travelled to Liverpool to embark on a troopship taking him back to Burma. All his private thoughts on the long voyage were centred on his 'sweet darling Audrey, because I love her so much. I shall be thrilled to get back to England so that I can marry her. I adore her so'. Many soldiers like him must have been similarly sustained during dark days in the jungle by thoughts of home and loved ones.

Above left: Audrey Harker in WRNS uniform, 1942. (Author's collection)

Above right: 'Tokyo Rose', Iva Toguri, an American-born Japanese woman, interviewed by American correspondents, September 1945.

'Tokyo Rose' was the generic name given by Allied troops in the Far East to all female English-speaking radio broadcasters of Japanese propaganda. She ceased to be a mere symbol in 1945 when Iva Toguri, an American-born Japanese woman, tried to return to America and was accused of being the real 'Tokyo Rose'. She was eventually tried and convicted of treason, but later pardoned, because it was realised that she had in fact worked to subvert the broadcasting of Japanese propaganda, and witnesses had been pressurised to speak out against her. By now she was sixty years old and lived out the rest of her life in Chicago, where she died in 2006. (Wikimedia Commons)

By the end of 1942 and at the beginning of 1943 the 17th Indian Division was fully mobilised and at full strength, reformed as a Light Division together with 48 and 63 Brigades, and proudly sporting its 'Black Cat' Badge. The scourge of malaria, 'flu, typhus and dysentery that had ravaged the army, had been brought under control with improved hygiene and drugs like Mepacrine, and as a result of their period of recuperation the division was now fit for combat. In 1943 the new Allied Command in South-East Asia (SEAC) was set up, with Admiral Lord Louis Mountbatten, aged forty-three, as Supreme Allied Commander. He set out on morale-boosting visits to the troops, with the four-fold message:

1. Stay and fight, supplied from the air. There will be no retreat.
2. We will not stop fighting when the monsoon comes.
3. We have anti-malaria measures and air-evacuation schemes so that we can fight in places like the Kabaw Valley, (a notorious malaria hotspot).
4. Who started this story about the Japanese superman? They can be beaten.

He integrated the Allied air forces in the area and authorised General Joseph Stilwell to develop a system of air transport from India over the Himalayas, ('The Hump'). The vital task was to increase the flow of supplies to the army in the field, so the Bengal-Assam Railway was taken over by the military, a regular air ferry 'Over the Hump' began, and an army of sappers built roads in Manipur, erected hospitals and built air strips. The roads from Palel to Tamu, and Imphal to Tiddim and on to Falam were painstakingly carved out of jungle and hillside. The task was largely completed without machinery and with

Admiral Lord Louis Mountbatten meeting men of the 17th Indian Division near Kennedy Peak, the 9,000-foot Japanese stronghold which lay across the XIVth Army's line of advance from Tiddim to the Chindwin River, 1944. (From *S.E.A.C. Souvenir Newspaper*, November 1944)

Heroic efforts were made to keep the troops entertained and maintain morale. A number of entertainers visited Burma, including Dame Vera Lynn. Here at an impromptu ENSA (Entertainments National Service Association) show, Carolyn Wright and Roberta Robertson are tap dancing on the dismantled top of a workbench, at Tabingaung airfield in Burma. The dancers and accordion accompanist had just survived an attack by Japanese aircraft, a reminder of the courage shown by the members of ENSA.

John Alexander, when writing home to his parents in 1943, included this humorous poem about ENSA.

> The ladies of ENSA appeal to the men, sir,
> There's no getting over the fact.
> From circle to stalls their beauty enthralls,
> When ENSA puts over an act.
>
> But when the show's ended, least said soonest mended,
> Just ponder on this one, my brothers.
> They won't have a spree with you or with me,
> They toddle straight home to their mothers!
>
> Or anyway that's what they say,
> I wonder if under the circs,
> It's just that they take a poor view,
> Of creatures like me and like you?

(© Imperial War Museum)

ingenuity and initiative. When they could not bring the materials they needed out of India the engineers built brick kilns along the route, and surfaced the road with home-made bricks, helped by Indian craftsmen (Slim, *Defeat into Victory* (Cassell, 1956), p. 172). Called 'Operation Navvy', the work was expected to take three months, and was mostly

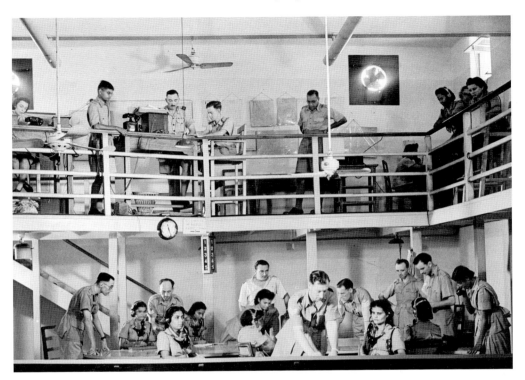

RAF Group Headquarters in North-East India, with RAF, India Air Force and Womens Auxiliary Corps personnel at work.

Air Marshall Sir Richard Pierce, AOC India and Ceylon, formed a new advanced Air Headquarters Bengal, based in Calcutta in close proximity to the army and naval command centres, in order to co-ordinate a response to the Japanese threat in Burma.

Squadrons of No. 221 Group, part of the RAF Third Tactical Air Force, gave vital air support to the XIVth Army during the crucial battles of Kohima and Imphal, and during the subsequent push back into Burma. General Slim's battle plan relied on air support and supply, and the victories and setbacks of the Allied forces in Burma largely reflect the degree of air superiority achieved. (© Imperial War Museum)

carried out by, among others, 60 Indian Light Field Company Queen Victoria's Own Madras Sappers and Miners, commanded by John Alexander. He commented:

> Never was the expression 'brute force and bloody ignorance' so apt, as all the work was carried out by hand in the most difficult terrain, with the road in my patch passing by Kennedy Peak, altitude 9,000 feet. The operation was completed ahead of schedule, and by the end of April 1943 jeeps were being ferried across the River Manipur. A pontoon was built and the battalion at Tiddim was being maintained by jeep. However, in May 1943 the Japanese attacked our forward positions and forced our troops to fall back on Fort White where 63 Brigade took over a defensive position throughout the rains. There followed months of guerilla warfare during which heavy casualties were inflicted on the Japanese. Guerrilla warfare by the local Chin tribespeople helped 63 Brigade to hold Kennedy Peak, the Kabaw Valley and Fort White, and to maintain dominance in the Chin Hills.

Objects: 9. Japanese Sword, 10. Good Luck Flags, 11. Japanese Uniform Badges, 12. John's Diary, 13. Black Cat Badge.

9. JAPANESE OFFICERS' SWORDS

Officers in the Japanese Army always wore a sword and frequently used it in battle. During the Meiji period in Japan (1868–1912) the ancient samurai class was disbanded and the carrying of swords in public was banned. Samurai armour and weapons were gradually replaced in the army by western-influenced uniforms and weapons. However, the Samurai ideal never died out, and during the years prior to the outbreak of the Second World War swords were once again produced on a large scale, and officers were required to wear a sword when they were on duty.

Alongside the old military swords (*Kyu gunto*), which were usually hand-forged and tempered in water, mass-produced swords (machine-made of inferior steel) were manufactured, called *showato*. The new military sword (*shin gunto*) was manufactured for the Japanese Army between 1935 and 1945 at the Toyokawa Naval Arsenal. This was a new style of sword designed in the style of a traditional tachi of the Kamakura Period (1185–1332), slung from the waist, with coloured tassels tied to a loop at the end of the hilt to indicate the rank of the wearer. Most of the blades were modern machine-produced, but some were traditionally manufactured or ancestral blades.

These swords were usually large, the blade about 71 cm in length, and the handle an additional 23 cm. The samurai sword represented the very essence of the ideology of Japanese militarism, a conscious link with the tradition of Bushido, the Samurai code of honour. Japanese military personnel used their swords, not just for ceremonial purposes, but in the thick of battle where hand-to-hand fighting was considered the most noble means of combat, and for the beheading of prisoners, or even their own soldiers found guilty of misconduct. Before the Japanese 33rd Division went into battle at Kohima their commanding officer General Mutaguchi told his troops that anyone guilty of misconduct must be punished: 'In order to keep bright the honour of his unit a Commander may have to use his sword as a weapon of execution, shameful though it may be to shed the blood of one's own soldiers on the battlefield...'

The swords that John Alexander brought back in his collection were taken from a Japanese officer who afterwards committed suicide by 'swallowing' a hand grenade. He would have considered this the only honourable way of redeeming the disgrace of becoming a prisoner of the enemy and surrendering his sword. These two swords remained in John's possession for many years, and were hurriedly photographed by his grandson Timothy before John's wife Audrey insisted that they should be handed over to the police to be destroyed, as she didn't want them in the house any longer. Thus two swords that had survived the rigours of the Burma Campaign, and which could have become family heirlooms, were lost to posterity. This photograph is the only record of them that survives.

10. JAPANESE GOOD LUCK FLAGS

Flag 1

This flag, showing a red disk on a white background, was known as the *Yosegaki hinomara*, a traditional gift for Japanese soldiers going off to fight in the Second World War. *Hinomara* means 'sun's circle', the red disc that was the national emblem, and *Yosegaki* means 'a collection of writing'. The writing often flowed out sideways, radiating from the sun, and was a combination of signatures of family members and friends, and short messages wishing the soldier good luck, all written with a calligraphy brush in black ink.

The *Hinomara*, or red sun, embodies the image of Japan as the land of the rising sun. The sun played an important part in Japanese mythology, because the Emperor was thought to be a direct descendant of the sun goddess Amaterasu, the chief deity of the Shinto religion. During the Meiji period (1868–1912) the sun disc and the Rising Sun Ensign of the Imperial Japanese Navy became major symbols of the emerging Japanese Empire.

On the right side of the flag is written '*Sanbo*', the martial arts code inherited from the Samurai Bushido, which says:

You must forget three things on the field of battle:
1) Remain alive and forget your family and home.
2) Devote yourself to your country's war and forget your parents and wife.
3) When you hear the sounds of battle, forget your body and your own life.

On the left-hand side of the flag are the words 'True Devotion', followed by the soldier's name 'Shoichi Yoshida'. The bottom line reads 'A wish for victory and good luck in the fortunes of war.' The flag is signed by the person who gave him the flag.

Dimensions: 84 cm x 74 cm.

Flag 2

The second flag is covered with the names, radiating out from the sun, of those family and friends saying farewell to Shoichi Yoshida, whose name appears across the top of the flag.

When Shoichi Yoshida was sent his 'red card', which drafted him into the armed forces, he proudly announced to his family, neighbours and friends that he had been honoured by the Emperor in being called up, and they responded by presenting him with this flag. On the right-hand side is a message wishing him good luck and hoping for his safety. The sun disc is surrounded by male names in the lower section and female names in the top section.

The flag offers the Bushido code as a spiritual shield urging soldiers to fight to the end, but also offering communal hopes and prayers for the owner every time the flag was unfolded. It was believed to provide a force or power that would see its owner through difficult times, and was worn under the tunic and close to the soldier's body.

Little effort was made to explain to soldiers or the civilian population of Japan why the war was being fought. Instead it was presented as a chance to rally round the Emperor, and as a purifying experience drawing the people back to the 'pure and cloudless heart' of the fundamental Japanese character, whose 'bright and strong' souls made them a superior race. Great honour attached to those who died in the service of the Emperor, because a belief in self-sacrifice was central to Japanese culture. Those who died in battle were treated as heroic 'gods of war'. Just as cherry blossom falls from the tree at the height of its beauty, so the warrior freely offered up his life to the Emperor.

Many of these flags were taken as souvenirs by Allied and American troops in the Burma Campaign and the war in the Pacific. Some are now finding their way back to descendants of those who fought, for whom there are no known graves and who are moved to be able to receive back these tangible links with their fathers or grandfathers.

Dimensions: 84 cm x 71 cm.

11. JAPANESE UNIFORM INSIGNIA

The usual uniform for regular troops consisted of a cotton tunic with open collar and two breast or waist pockets, worn with trousers or shorts, and on the head a lightweight cotton field cap with a four-flap sun curtain.

The trousers were a lightweight version of standard breeches worn tucked into puttees, in various colours ranging from khaki to dark jungle green.

Regular troops wore brown pigskin ankle boots, while officers wore high brown boots or leather gaiters and ankle boots. Variations of uniform were largely dictated by wartime shortages, and by the latter stages of the conflict soldiers uniforms had become very ragged and threadbare, as no supplies were getting through and the ordinary soldier had to repair his own uniform.

Insignia
Officers wore rhomboid-shaped collar patches on which were displayed stars of rank. The badges in John Alexander's collection are from a Second-Lieutenant (red cloth, brown edging, gold stripe and silver star), a Corporal (red cloth, brown edging, yellow stripe and star – rectangular), a Superior Private (red cloth, three yellow stars), and a 2nd Class Private (red cloth, one yellow star). These badges suggest that they were taken from four different soldiers.

Dimensions: 4.5 cm x 2.5 cm.

12. JOHN ALEXANDER'S SERVICE DIARY

This small pocket diary, covered in blue cloth with the name 'The Services Diary' and the emblems of the Army, Air Force and Navy on the front, was published by the Army Sport Control Board, and was available from stationers shops or the NAAF Institute. The diary covers the period from the end of 1941 to the end of 1942. John spent most of this time in recuperation and training in England at Aldershot Barracks, but seems to have been able to see his girlfriend Audrey Harker on most days after work. Throughout the long days in camp and the often boring routine of army life, it was his developing relationship with Audrey that kept John stable and happy. But eventually his leave ended and he was called back, and in November he boarded the troop train for Liverpool, embarking from the docks on 16 December for the long passage to India. Every diary entry during the voyage mentions John's love for Audrey, especially on 22 December, which was a particularly difficult day for John, because it was Audrey's birthday. She was just twenty years old. 'I was miserable and missed Audrey terribly. I went to bed early and slept dreaming of Audrey, my angel.'

Dimensions: 11.25 cm x 7.5 cm.

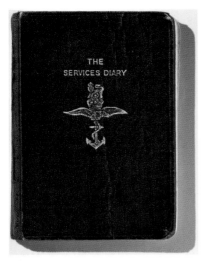
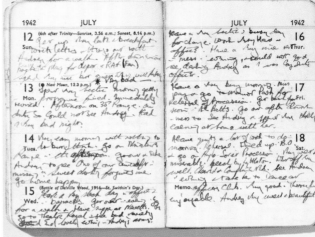

13. THE BLACK CAT BADGE

When John Alexander arrived back in India early in 1942 after his period of leave, he discovered that the symbol of the 17th Indian Division had been changed from 'Streak of Lightening' to the famous 'Black Cat' badge, showing a black cat with arched back against a yellow background. This was the emblem by which the division was known for the rest of the campaign. There is a story that this decision was taken after the Japanese radio propagandist, whom the Allies nicknamed 'Tokyo Rose', had been sneering at the division in her broadcasts as 'the division whose sign is a yellow streak', referring to its ignominious retreat through Burma. The black cat, by contrast, was both a symbol of luck and of defiance, a sign that the 17th Indian Division was made of sterner stuff, and that its luck was definitely about to change. John wore his 'Black Cat' badge proudly and brought it home with him stained as it was with jungle dirt and human blood, a tangible symbol of all he had had to endure in the service of his country.

Dimensions: 5.5 cm x 5.5 cm.

Chapter V

Fighting Back

The Southern Front

Meanwhile, on the Southern Front, after an initial disastrous campaign to retake the Mayu peninsula in the Arakan, the Allies launched a second offensive in late 1943, on the broken coastline of jungle-covered hills covered by deep river valleys. The Japanese

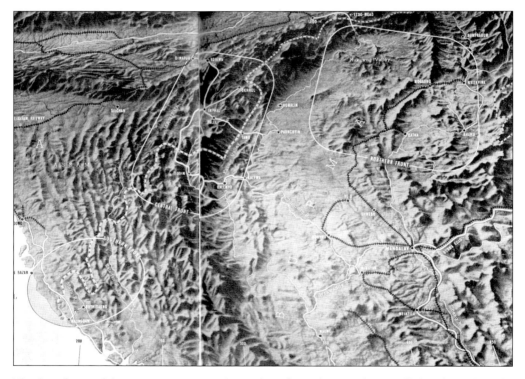

The three fronts of the Burma Campaign. The southern front, the coastal strip called Arakan where the Japanese forces tried to break through to Calcutta; when this failed they switched their attack to the central front, which culminated in the battles of Imphal and Kohima; while on the northern front General Stilwell pushed his Ledo Road south past Myitkyina to link up with the Burma Road. (HMSO, 1946)

The West Tunnel on the Maungdaw–Buthidaung road looking towards Maungdaw on the Naaf River Estuary, just visible in the distance. (© Imperial War Museum)

General Sakurai struck in force at the Allied positions, trapping the 7th Indian Division in Sinzweya, but they held out, and fought back in what came to be known as the Battles of the Admin Box, 'Okeydoke Pass' and the Maungdaw-Buthidaung Tunnels. Supplies poured in from the air and by sea into Maungdaw, and reinforcements in the shape of the 26th Indian Division came in down the Chittagong Road. Although the fighting was incredibly fierce, and the Japanese brutal and merciless, regularly putting on hoods and hideous face masks and slithering through the tiger grass uttering weird animal calls to try to terrify their opponents, the Allied forces stood firm. The Japanese were trapped between the Allied divisions, short of food and ammunition, with their timetable in ruins. The British Prime Minister Winston Churchill sent a message to the 14th Army: 'The enemy has been challenged and beaten in jungle warfare. His boastfulness has received a salutary exposure.'

The Northern Front

Another Allied operation that helped to puncture notions of Japanese superiority was conducted by Major-General Orde Wingate, who organised a guerilla force, the 77th Indian Infantry Brigade, ('The Chindits'), for the purposes of long range penetration behind enemy lines to create havoc and disrupt enemy communications and supplies. They secretly advanced into Burma from Imphal in February 1943, with the objective of cutting the main railway lines between Mandalay, Myitkyina and Lashio.

Chindit Operations behind Japanese lines. Chindits place explosive charges on a railway bridge in 1944. (© Imperial War Museum)

The Japanese were caught by surprise and left confused, not knowing the intentions of the Chindits or how numerous they were. Eventually they discovered that the force was of brigade strength, and was being supplied by air drops, and the Japanese sent three regiments to the area to destroy them. On 24 March Wingate was ordered to withdraw, and the force, by now deep in enemy territory, scattered into several columns to make their way to safety in India or China.

John Tulloch, posted to Palel with RAF 2943 Squadron, as a Wireless Operator, was one of a small platoon of Special Forces attached to the North Western Frontier Forces, tasked with infiltrating behind Japanese lines in an attempt to find some of Wingate's Chindits and get them out to safety. Their route began somewhere between Imphal and Palel. They were lightly armed, dressed in green jungle dress, armed with a Sten gun and a knife, their belts festooned with half a dozen hand grenades. They had one blanket and a ground sheet between two men, a light mosquito net, a haversack with rations, and a Bren gun carried by the officer leading the column. For extra food and clothing they relied on air drops. In an account written after the war John Tulloch described some of their experiences:

> We wandered around for three days and it was a rare piece of luck that we ran into no Japs or I might not have been here to write this. On the morning of the second day my side-kick Frank and I got up from under the one blanket and went off on our own to do a scrounge. I still have no idea what we were looking for, food, water, or just to pass the time, who knows, perhaps we smelled wood burning, I cannot remember. We followed an animal track for quite some distance in the grey light of early morning until we came to a clearing in the jungle. In the centre were a couple of huts that

John Tulloch in RAF uniform, 1940. (Joyce and Leslie Howard)

had been built Naga fashion, and a thin trickle of smoke issued from underneath the eaves of one. The first thought in our minds was 'Japs', so we hid and waited. Sure enough a Jap Officer appeared in the doorway and scratched himself, then went back inside again. We waited for some signs of others but there seemed to be none. I have wondered since, why that one Jap officer was there on his own. At the time the Japs were on the run and heading for Tamu in the Kabaw Valley, therefore like us he may have got lost and was having a night's kip in the abandoned hut.

After about fifteen minutes Frank and I took courage and laid a scheme. I would take the end door and Frank the side door and rush in blazing with our Sten guns at the same time. As I crept through the undergrowth my heart was in my mouth. Although I do not suppose I made any noise louder than a mouse would have made, it seemed to me that I was crashing around like a full grown elephant. Nearer and nearer I crept keeping my eyes on that door and having a quick glance now and again to see how Frank was progressing. Gauging our distance, nearer and nearer the doors we slowly worked our way, then when we were about five yards from our respective doors we made a terrific dash in through the doors and opened fire. That Jap Officer never knew what hit him; in fact the weight of lead entering his body nearly drove him through the wall.

About ten days after the Jap Officer incident in the hut, we were making our way back from the Chindwin Valley towards Tamu. We had not found any of Major Wingate's men. Early one morning Frank and I were out on the scrounge once more. This time we were after clean water. Owing to the constant rains every stream, river and pool had turned to a yellow muddy torrent unfit to drink, so we were out in search of some spring or pool that was more or less clean, but with little hope of finding one.

British troops move forward in thick jungle in Burma, 1944. (Wikipedia Commons)

The jungle here was riddled with tracks and paths, Naga paths, Jap paths, animal paths. We were wandering from one to the other aimlessly, but always on the alert. Veering from one to another around a bend we came across two Japs sound asleep under one blanket, nothing but their heads sticking out. Whether they were alive or dead we couldn't quite make out for a little while as we watched them, a Sten gun at the ready. One moved a little, they were alive; slowly we crept up to them until we were close enough to ascertain that they were sound asleep. Right up to them we slowly worked our way until we were standing one at each side of their lowly bed. With one accord Frank and I detached a hand grenade from our belts and pulled the pin. Holding the grenades in our right hands we grasped the corners of the blanket carefully with our left hands, lifted it up a fraction and threw the grenades underneath shouting 'wakie-wakie', and dashing back into the jungle, flung ourselves flat on our stomachs. There was a crash, a yell and then a flailing of limbs. We did not go back to see the results, and it did not take us many minutes to put a considerable distance between ourselves and the scene. Back in camp we were asked, 'What in hell's name had we been up to?' But Frank and I never divulged our episode with the grenades that morning while in search of clean water. In the jungle the rule you lived by was 'Kill or be Killed'.

Of the 3,000 officers and men of the Chindits who went into Burma behind Japanese lines only 2,182 came back, in poor physical condition but elated that they had managed to cause some mischief and tie up a considerable number of enemy troops who had to be diverted from other operations. Wingate had proved that long range penetration could work, shown the success of using air supply drops for maintaining jungle operations, and most importantly proved that Allied troops could take on the Japanese at jungle warfare and win.

Later, in March 1944, Operation Thursday brought 10,000 glider troops from India and set them down across the Mandalay–Myitkyina railway. Their job was to disrupt the enemy's supply and so lessen resistance to General Joseph Stilwell, who was fighting south down the Ledo Road. In May 'Merrill's Marauders', a long-range deep penetration group under Brigadier-General Frank Merrill seized the airfield at Myitkyina and later the town itself was captured. From August 1944 the Allied 36 Division struck south down the 'railway corridor' from Mogaung, carrying troops and equipment forward and eventually linking up with the 19th Indian Division in December. They crossed the Irrawaddy and the advance southward continued. The liberation of northern Burma had begun.

Brigadier Orde Wingate after returning from operations in Japanese-occupied Burma with the Chindits in 1943.
  Wingate was an eccentric and unconventional soldier, who wore an old pith helmet, let his beard grow to save time, ate raw onions, and quoted Aristotle, Plato and the Old Testament. Although regarded with suspicion by many, his determination to take the offensive and get behind enemy lines impressed Prime Minister Winston Churchill, who supported the formation of his long-range penetration commando force, the Chindits.
(© Imperial War Museum)

An aerial view of the Ledo Road during the campaign in North and Central Burma, February to August 1944.

The Ledo Road was an overland route between India and China, built during the Burma Campaign to enable supplies to be delivered to China. It was masterminded by General Jo Stilwell after the Burma Road between Lashio and Yunnan was cut off in 1942 by the Japanese forces, and renamed the Stilwell Road. After Rangoon was captured by the Japanese and before the Ledo Road was finished, the majority of supplies to the Chinese had to be delivered by airlift over the eastern end of the Himalayas known as 'The Hump'. (© Imperial War Museum)

Operation Thursday, March 1944. American transport aircraft towing gliders that carry Chindit forces who will prepare the airstrips behind enemy lines for aircraft. (© Imperial War Museum)

Chapter VI

The Central Front

On the Central Front of the campaign, because of the continuing strengthening of Japanese forces, the 17th Indian Division was ordered to abandon the Chin Hills and move to Imphal in March 1944. The Japanese Army, commanded by General Masakazu Kawabe, comprised three separate armies: 28 Army under Shozo Sakurai, 15 Army

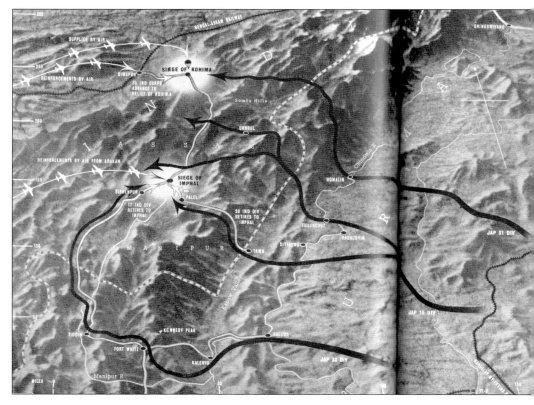

Map of the Central Front. In March 1944 a Japanese Army, 100,000 strong, struck west across the Chindwin River. The Allies withdrew to the Imphal Plain, and fought back there and at Kohima, supplied from the air. After months of hard fighting the enemy were in retreat, and the Allies began to advance back across the Chindwin and to push south. (HMSO, 1946)

under Renya Mutaguchi, and 33 Army under Masaki Honda. Each army consisted of three divisions, although some were considerably understrength, and their supply lines were by now stretched to the limit. The Japanese plan for the 15th Army, 'Operation U-Go', had three objectives:

1. To cross the frontier and seize the Allied base at Imphal.
2. To cut the Bengal-Assam railway, which was the lifeline for General Stilwell's troops, and force him to retreat to Ledo.
3. To overrun the Assam airfields, disrupting traffic over 'the Hump' into China, thus cutting off communications and forcing China out of the war.

In the face of this threat General Slim decided to withdraw his troops from the frontier to the Imphal plain and meet the Japanese forces there. The plain lies 3,000 feet up in the heart of the Manipur mountains, about 300 square miles in area, entered from India by the north via Dimapur, Kohima and down into the valley. The crucial advantage enjoyed by the Allies was that by March 1944 they had established air superiority, both in terms of attack from the air, and of bringing in supplies. This would be a crucial factor in the battles ahead.

The 17th Indian Division covered the approaches to Tiddim, under Major-General 'Punch' Cowan. The Japanese 33rd Division under General Mutaguchi approached from the south to attack Imphal in four columns, whose respective objectives were:

1. To attack straight up the road from Kalewa to Tamu.
2. To circle round Tiddim and cut the road from the south.
3. To march west from the Chindwin to cut the Tiddim Road.
4. To move straight up the Tiddim Road.

Major-General D. T. ('Punch') Cowan, Commander, 17th Indian Division. He had been Director of Military Training in India from 1941 to 1942, but was appointed CO of the 17th Indian Division when its previous commander Jackie Smyth was relieved after ordering the bridge over the Sittang River to be blown in February 1942. He remained in command of the division for the rest of the Burma Campaign. (From *S.E.A.C. Souvenir Newspaper*, November 1944)

Milestone 109 on the Tiddim Road where the Japanese cut the road behind the 17th Indian Division in March 1944 and where they subsequently established a supply dump, which was heavily bombed by the RAF. (© Imperial War Museum)

They pressed hard upon the Allied outposts around Kennedy Peak and moved in an arc from the south towards the 17th Division, which withdrew, booby-trapping the area, and leaving Tiddim in flames. The Japanese tried to slice up the columns of the 17th Division along the trail by throwing roadblocks across the road, but the Allied gunners blasted away at them and the infantry and transport followed. The 23rd Division arrived just in time to reinforce the attack, allowing the 17th Division to escape the enemy and march on to Imphal.

Immediately on arrival 63 Brigade was brought straight back into battle to counter a threat against the airfield and to hold positions at Tamu and along the Tiddim Road, which stretched northwards from Tiddim village in the Chin Hills right up to Imphal. General Slim in his book *Defeat into Victory* commented that here and on the Silchar to Bishenpur Track some of the heaviest fighting in the entire Imphal-Kohima battle took place. The Japanese 33rd Imperial Guards Division was probably the toughest division in Burma, and although reduced in numbers, exhausted and short of supplies, they delivered a series of furious assaults with supreme courage and tenacity. 63 Brigade moved to Bishenpur on 7 May 1944, and were involved in fierce engagements at Potsangbam, which resulted in the capture of Kha Aimol, a mountain village on the route used by the Japanese to approach the Silchar-Bishenpur Track from the west.

John Alexander, in a letter home to his parents, described his part in this attack:

It was 6 o'clock. There was a hum of activity prevailing. The preparations for yet another 'job' were underway. Sapper equipment was being packed very carefully onto the mules and padded with sackcloth to prevent any noise. Even the feet of the mules were padded – for tonight surprise was essential. Some men were loading, others putting bare necessities into their packs and tying their blankets around the outside, and the rest – the N.C.O.s – were getting final instructions from their platoon officer.

At last all was ready, and we were about to move off when one of the mules trod on his halter, and started off without the party. Ten minutes was wasted which had to be picked up on the march. The first part of the march was along the dusty earthbound road that was our main line of communication, our one link with civilisation. After a six mile march the sappers arrived at the rendezvous point and waited, not daring to do anything but breathe. A cigarette meant a bullet or a shell. Yet finally looking down the road one could see a blurred shadow and a faint slide of army boots as the infantry moved up. We merged and moved on. I must confess I felt much safer now in the centre of a brigade.

We soon left the road and moved in open formation across the paddy, and it was here that I nearly lost one section, moving across open paddy at night with no moon, no noise. Two large streams were crossed and when everyone was wet up to the waist it rained and we got all the rest wet. As yet the sons of Nippon had not shown any activity. We hoped that we had not been discovered. And so it went on until our first objective was reached – a small village. It was completely unoccupied (our suspicions were roused). Anyway we were able to take a rest for a few hours, and still nothing happened.

Sometime after midnight we started off again and advanced across more paddy fields towards the line of hills held by the Japs. Dawn broke suddenly upon our foot-weary brigade and a halt was ordered in a basin near the foot of these hills. Defences were dug and the day soon passed. We were glad of the night once again for the Japs had registered us and things were beginning to become a little uncomfortable.

That night two battalions were sent off into the hills to take two strong-points overlooking our position, and my platoon of sappers was detailed as the 'assault' platoon.

Sometime later I was wakened from my slumber by intensive firing, shortly followed by an excited sapper shouting in my ear 'Dushiaan. Enge' (the enemy is here – Tamil). So I ordered a charge – keeping as far behind as possible myself! We surprised one section of Japs and made rather a mess of their ranks, adding one knotch to my kukri and another to my 'tommy gun' (the same gun used by the gunner who was killed by my side in P –). Having over-run this post we continued down the valley but meeting no more opposition we returned to an ambush. Luckily it was spotted and the Jap fired too late. We beat a hasty retreat and rejoined the brigade but by another route.

Next morning dawned and being sappers we had to start work on the track and get supplies through – supplies that never came. The road had been blocked behind us. We were used to this by now and the next three days on half scale rations were accomplished. My orderly saved my life – or my stomach – by producing a tin of bully beef. I ate it without question. The track was finished in spite of the rain which poured down on us unceasingly for ten days. Being wet was more unpleasant than being hungry. Soon after the road block was cleared and supplies reached us. Operations ceased while we had our first good hot meal in three days. Even the rain stopped for a few hours. All was peace and quiet in the fox-hole.

Then the shelling started in real earnest. The rain beat down in equal earnest. This latest outburst by the Jap gunners made us move up into the hills and after a long and hazardous climb we entered and occupied the village of Kha Aimol. Unlike our comrades in the west, all that was left to greet us in this liberated village were the pi-dogs and the smell of rotting corpses. The village – although tactically advantageous – literally 'stank'.

The next day was spent building a brigade water point and continuing the track up to our new position, a job which eventually turned out to be impossible. The heavy rains had swelled the river and stream so that they not only flowed into the paddy fields but over the banks (the banks between the fields over which the roads were constructed). With the help of bridges constructed from ammunition boxes and old beds and doors from the village a road was started – and washed away the next day. What a life!

But we did get a mule track up to our forward positions in spite of the rain. Water is the sapper's worst enemy. He either has to bridge it, produce it or get rid of it. Owing to the suddenness of the move, we were left in peace for about 18 hours. But during the next day the Japs had discovered our main position and made it as uncomfortable as possible for us. One Jap section was discovered that morning sitting just outside our wire digging in! As soon as we opened up all ran straight down the hill leaving tools, arms and three dead comrades behind. Two battalions, with sapper assault demolition parties were sent to clear the Japs from the hills around our village and destroy their guns. This was done in two days, and then we felt safe.

Our sapper demolition party on completion of its job was on it's way back when it saw a Jap mule convoy coming along an adjacent ridge. An ambush position was taken and the convoy just fell into the bag. Once again the muleteers just ran when the sappers opened up. Unfortunately the light machine gun had been left in camp so only two dead Japs were left with their mules. The mules, which turned out to be donkeys, were led back to our lines and the spoil examined. Besides biscuits and other dry rations we found two medical panniers and two stone jars of 'saki' (the Japs' 'rum' ration).

By now the brigade was feeling very tired and ill. We had not had a rest for six months and everyone was wondering when all this would finish. I had an attack of colitis, followed by a bout of fever which in the evening rose to a temperature of 103°, brought on by the inflammation of 'jungle sores'. The Brigadier refused me permission to go sick when I was once caught in my bunker too weak to move, and ordered me back to work below on the track. I was the only sapper officer in the Brigade and could not go back until relieved. After three days of fever, etc., I was relieved by the company – but my weary men had to stay on. The brigade was still fighting – it had to hold on for another week. And it did. When the brigade eventually pulled out we only left the Japs with two guns and one company to follow us up. But we had done our job and held him for three weeks. The big push had started when we got back, and the brigade ate and slept for two days.

A week earlier I was 'evacuated' to hospital. With a temperature of only 99° one morning I was sent back to the jeep point. I was a walking casualty, but the five miles took me three hours. Men could not be spared to go with me so I just carried on up through Jap country with nothing save my clothes and toothbrush! Eventually I reached the nulla and waited for a jeep. I was hoisted up into the jeep some half an hour later, and thanks to the American driver made as comfortable as possible. The bumping of the jeep over corduroy roads made me sick and really ill and I arrived at

A wounded soldier is taken by jeep to hospital at Imphal. (From 'Into Burma' Magazine, Inter-Services Public Relations Directorate, GHQ, New Delhi)

the Advanced Dressing Station with a temperature of 104°., finishing the journey to hospital on a stretcher. Here my clothes were condemned, I was 'deloused' and put into bed. Two days later, clad only in hospital pijamas, boots and a blanket I was flown to a base hospital.

In spite of many casualties the attacks of the Japanese 33rd Division were repulsed. Most of their guns and tanks had been destroyed, and starvation and disease had seriously reduced their fighting capacity. Kha Aimol had been held, the Tiddim Road was secured, and 63 Brigade entered Thinnungyi unopposed. From July 1944 the whole of 17th Division withdrew for rest, reorganisation and re-equipment to Ranchi in India, and John Alexander was granted three weeks leave. He flew home to spend the time in Reigate and London, conscious that the honour of the 17th Indian Division had to a large extent been restored.

Our long duel with the 33rd Japanese Division was over. We had been opposed to them since January 1942, and now we had smashed them. The 17th Indian Division had been in action continuously for thirty-one months, in the course of which four soldiers of the Division had been awarded the Victoria Cross.

Meanwhile, the Japanese 31st Division drove forward towards Kohima, and swept round it expecting the Allies to retreat or surrender. They did neither, instead standing firm and defending stoutly. The small isolated garrison of 3,500 men were besieged by

Aerial view of Imphal-Kohima battle area, March–July 1944. Imphal area looking north. (© Imperial War Museum)

15,000 Japanese, but they stood fast for sixty-four days. The road from Dimapur climbs tortuously up a valley to a saddle 5,000 feet high called Kohima Ridge, along which are a number of hillocks that the garrison at Kohima held, surrounded by commanding heights. The battle, which was prolonged, bloody and often fought hand to hand to and fro over the length of the District Commissioner's garden, has been described many times in great detail. Having been forced into the tiny area called 'Summerhouse' or 'Garrison Hill', the garrison held on and was eventually relieved by an assault on Gun Spur, after which the Japanese forces abandoned the ridge. The battle had lasted sixty-four days. The Commander of the Japanese 31st Division, Lieutenant-General Koboku Sato, had given the order to his troops: 'You will fight to the death. When you are killed you will fight on with your spirit.' But by now the Japanese were sick, starving and short of supplies, with over 7,000 dead. The 33 Corps pursued the retreating Japanese, with the British 2nd Division advancing down the main road, and the 7th Indian Division moving in parallel to the east. On 22 June the British 2nd Division met the main body of the 5th Indian Infantry Division advancing north from Imphal, 30 miles south of Kohima, thus opening the road to truck convoys that carried vital supplies to the troops on the Imphal Plain.

The battles of Imphal and Kohima were the greatest battles of the jungle war, and are rightly remembered to this day. The spine of the Japanese Imperial Army in South-East Asia was broken, and the enemy was now on the defensive, with greatly reduced and weakened forces strewn out along the Imphal Road. Brigades of the 7th Indian Division drove eastwards towards Ukhrul, the Japanese mountain base between the Imphal Road and the Chindwin River, while other units pressed north-eastwards

View of Garrison Hill battlefield after Battle of Kohima, March–July 1944. Garrison Hill was the key to the British defences. (© Imperial War Museum)

Above: View of Kohima Ridge after the battle, March–July 1944. (© Imperial War Museum)

Right: Graves of soldiers killed in the long and bloody battle for Kohima. (From 'Into Burma' Magazine, GHQ, New Delhi)

The Madras Sappers and Miners on the road called the 'Jessami Track', 30 miles to the east of Kohima. (From 'Into Burma' Magazine, GHQ, New Delhi)

to crush Japanese forces there. The Japanese 33rd Division under General Mutaguchi, had planned with their three-pronged attack to break into India in ten days and their supply lines were based on that calculation, but the Allies had wrought havoc with this timetable, and as a result the condition of the enemy had deteriorated badly. They lacked food, medical supplies and fresh ammunition. Many suffered from beri-beri, and were abandoned or killed by their own troops as the Japanese withdrew towards the Chindwin River.

Many years later some of the Japanese soldiers who took part in the retreat set down their experiences, which were collected in a book *Tales by Japanese Soldiers*, edited by Kazuo Tamayama and John Nunneley (Weidenfeld and Nicholson, 1992). One soldier, Staff Sargeant Yasumasa Nishiji, recorded:

> Those struggling along the road were almost all in their twenties, yet they stooped like old men. The sight was one of total misery ... It became a routine that a soldier who was emaciated and crippled, with no hope of recovery, was given a grenade and persuaded, without words, to sort himself out ... It often occurred that soldiers took their own lives in pairs. They embraced, placing a grenade between them. We called it double suicide.

The victories at Kohima and Imphal had spoiled the Japanese dream of reaching India. As General Slim told his troops at the time:

> 'The Japanese will never come back. In this year we have thrashed the Japanese soldier, man for man, and decisively. Next year we shall smash the Japanese Army.'

* * * * * * * * * * * * *

While resting at Ranchi the 17th Indian Division was reorganised. They ceased to be a Light Division and became a mechanised division ready for the recapture of Burma.

At the end of November 1944 the division left Ranchi and returned to Imphal, arriving in January 1945. It was reported officially that 'the Division arrived fresh, well-equipped, self-confident and thankful to be back!' How far these feelings were shared by the rank and file is hard to guess!

While the 17th Indian Division had been recuperating and reorganising at Ranchi, the XIVth Army drove eastwards, pushing the Japanese from Kennedy Peak and Fort White, down to Kalemyo. The 19th Indian Division ('The Dagger Division') forced a crossing of the Chindwin and linked up with Allied columns from the north, establishing a bridgehead on 3 December 1944 at Kalewa. It was a symbolic occasion, because here, two and a half years earlier, General Slim had led the British rearguard over the Chindwin River in retreat. From August the 36th Division had been marching down the 'railway corridor' from Mogaung, using the railway to carry troops and equipment forward. On 16 December they linked up with the 19th Indian Division, crossed the Irrawaddy and advanced southwards. In the east the Chinese Expeditionary Force was pushing westwards to Bhamo from Yunnan, and by January 1945 had forced its way through to link up with the Northern Combat Area Command, and on 27 January the road from India through Burma into China was reopened. The push southwards by the Allies to recapture Mandalay and Rangoon had begun.

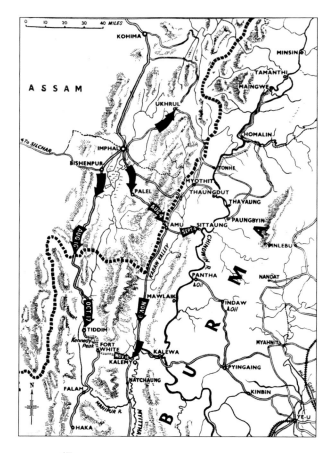

Map of the Allied advance after the battles of Imphal and Kohima, May to November 1944. (From *S.E.A.C. Souvenir Newspaper*, November 1944)

Above: A view of the 1,1000-foot Bailey Bridge across the Chindwin River as it nears completion, less than twelve hours after the XIVth Army captured Kalewa, 2 December 1944. (© Imperial War Museum)

Left: Two soldiers of the South Wales Borderers patrolling through dust and rubble in front of the Bahe Pagoda, Central Burma.

They were part of the 36th Division, which had fought its way down the railway corridor from Myitkyina to Mandalay before capturing the village of Bahe in January 1945. (© Imperial War Museum)

Objects: 14. Japanese Cigarettes, 15. Japanese Ammo and Knife, 16. Chopsticks.

14. KOOA CIGARETTES

During the Second World War cigarettes were distributed free to soldiers and often included in their rations. Soldiers were encouraged to smoke both to relieve boredom and to improve morale. Because of the development of mass-produced cigarettes from the 1880s onwards, cigarette companies sent thousands of free boxes to the various theatres of war to generate publicity for their brands. Japanese soldiers were no exception to this, particularly as about 80 per cent of Japanese adults were regular smokers by 1941. Cigarettes were not regarded as a luxury but seen as part of everyday life. They were the most frequently requested comfort item by serving soldiers, and a range of brands was produced, including 'Golden Bat', *'Asahi'* ('rising sun'), *'Dai Asia'* ('Great Asia'), 'Heron', *'Kyukko'* ('Polar Lights'), and the brand illustrated here, *'Kooa'* ('Asia Reconstruction').

Kooa cigarettes were made in Cirebon, Java, in Indonesia, from Virginian tobacco, and supplied to military bases. Japanese soldiers received five packets of *Kooa* cigarettes per month. Each packet contained twenty cigarettes, and the illustration shows a heavy-duty brown paper wrapper with three packets still inside. Perhaps the carton originally contained twenty packets because the label on the front has the number 400 printed on it. The Imperial War Museum in London has a packet of *Kooa* cigarettes donated by a former prisoner from the notorious Changi Jail in Singapore, where cigarettes were valuable and much sought-after currency.

Dimensions: 7 cm x 5 cm.

15. JAPANESE RIFLE AMMUNITION AND KNIFE

In an envelope that John Alexander brought back from Burma were six rounds of what were described on the envelope as '.256 Rifle Ammunition', together with two spent bullets. The main armament used by the Japanese Army in the Second World War was the Type 38 Arisaka Rifle, which used a 6.5 mm x 50 mm cartridge, which was designated in British military circles 'the .256 inch', representing the bore diameter of the rifle.

The Arisaka Rifle is a type of Japanese bolt-action service rifle that was in production from 1897 until the end of the Second World War, designed originally by Colonel Arisaka Nariakira

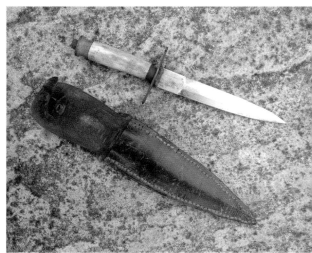

(1852–1915). The Type 38 was developed by Major Nambu Kÿiro in 1905, and nearly 3.5 million were manufactured. It proved to be a good and reliable combat rifle, with practically no recoil and good accuracy up to about 500 yards, but with its bayonet attached it was a long and unwieldy weapon for Japanese troops of small stature. On some occasions, when preparing to attack the enemy, Japanese soldiers were ordered to adopt the traditional mode of combat in which they were forbidden to load bullets into their rifles, told to smear mud on their bayonets to prevent them from glinting in the sun, and charge the enemy positions using only their bayonets as weapons.

The bayonet knife or fighting knife is a short weapon, 22 cm in length, with a bone handle in a leather sheath 26 cm long, with a strap to hold the handle in place. Presumably it was worn on a belt around the waist and used in close-combat fighting.

16. JAPANESE IVORY CHOPSTICKS

The Japanese were proud of their diet, and rice was believed to be part of the very heart of Japanese civilisation. Polished white rice was considered to be more desirable than rice still in husks, even though this had additional nutritional benefit. The Japanese attributed their physical and mental strength to their plain frugal diet. Labourers would work a whole day on a diet of tomatoes, cucumber, salad and rice, but one of the results was a propensity to the disease of beriberi, a thiamine deficiency due to a lack of vitamin B, which became particularly marked and critical among troops fighting in the South-East Asia theatres of war.

During the late nineteenth century it had been discovered that by mixing barley with rice beriberi could almost be eradicated. Barley was often mixed with the rice supplied to the troops, but frequently soldiers separated out the barley and discarded it. Rations were supplied to the army in bulk, sent to Field Supply Depots, from where they were transported to supply points in the combat area. Here they were issued to the troops as 'A Rations' and 'B Rations'. 'A Rations' consisted of a two-day supply of uncooked, polished rice, canned meat, and cooking fuel, all packed in a bamboo tube. 'B Rations' consisted of one hundred pieces of hard tack in a cloth wrapper and canned meat.

The rice was cooked by the soldiers themselves, usually in designated areas, but often the smoke from their fires gave away their position in the jungle. Soldiers going into combat were supplied with packets of small hard biscuits (*Kanpan*), cakes of compressed barley, dried fish, plums or prunes, which could be mixed with water and made into a hot cereal. The Japanese soldier carried a mess kit consisting of a tin carrier with tray and cover. Supplementary rations included cigarettes, *saké* and sweets. Clearly some soldiers preferred to use chopsticks rather than eating with their hands, and this object is a fine pair of ivory chopsticks, 26 cm long.

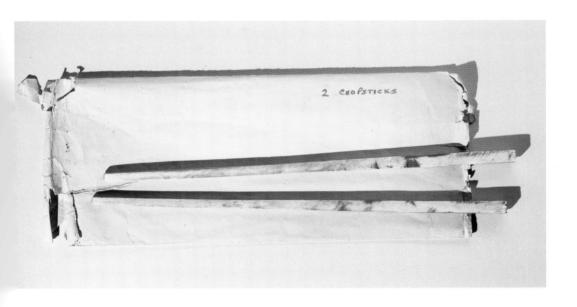

Chapter VII

Elephant Man

John Alexander's main role in this ongoing conflict was as an engineer, or 'sapper', working to build roads through the jungle, and bridges across the rivers. This was hard and unremitting work, often using the local labour force in addition to the regular troops. About 72,000 engineers and 130,000 labourers, equivalent to the ration strength of a dozen infantry divisions, kept the XIVth Army moving forward, and the vital supplies and ammunition coming through. In this task every variety of transport was pressed into service, including, mules, oxen and even elephants. Elephants had for many years been employed in the vast teak forests of Burma, and during the campaign they became a vital tool in the engineers' armoury. The Allies used elephants less for transport than for road and bridge building, because an elephant can lay a plank or a log with the precision of a carpenter. As General Slim commented:

> In the XIVth Army … the elephant held a special place in our esteem. It was not, I think, a matter of size and strength. It was the elephant's dignity and intelligence that gained our real respect. To watch an elephant building a bridge, to see the skill with which the great beast lifted the huge logs and the accuracy with which they were coaxed into position, was to realise that the trained elephant was no mere transport animal, but indeed a skilled sapper.
>
> I could never judge myself how much of this uncanny skill was the elephant's own and how much his rider's. Obviously it was the combination of the two which produced the result, and without the brave, cheerful, patient, loyal Burmese oozie our elephant companies could not have existed. And we should have had no oozies had it not been for men like 'Elephant Bill' and his assistants. It was their jungle craft, elephant sense, dogged courage, and above all the example they set, which held the Elephant Companies together under every stress that war, terrain and climate could inflict on them.

The 'Elephant Bill' Slim refers to was Lieutenant-Colonel James Howard Williams, who had been working for the Bombay Burma Trading Corporation as a forestry assistant looking after elephants. In October 1942 he joined the staff of the XIVth Army as 'Elephant Adviser', and was in demand to provide elephants for the Royal Engineers to help build bridges. Eventually this Elephant Transport Company was officially handed over to the Royal Engineers, and by the beginning of 1944 they were based at Tamu helping to improve the main road from Tamu to Kalemyo, using Bailey and Hamilton bridges. The elephants delivered 2,300 tons of timber at the road in three months.

Because of the rapid Japanese advance towards the Chindwin River in 1944 Williams was ordered to collect all the available elephants, about eighty in all, and get them out of the Kabaw Valley. When the Japanese launched their offensive against the 17th Indian Division, Williams took his remaining elephants over the hills towards Imphal, and then on over the mountains to a tea plantation, Baledan, in Assam. While the battles for Kohima and Imphal were raging, for four months Williams kept his elephants together in readiness for a push back into Burma with the XIVth Army against the Japanese. After the victory at Imphal Williams brought them back, and as the Allies advanced down the Tiddim Road, the elephants were used to build bridges and keep the roads and tracks to the Chindwin repaired, as the Allies poured back into Burma.

Williams attached parties of elephants, with their 'oozies', to sapper companies, with one officer responsible for their supervision. John Alexander was one of these officers, and soon established a strong bond with his elephants. After the war Williams wrote a book about his exploits, (J. H. Williams, *Elephant Bill*, 1950), in which he singled out John Alexander for particular mention:

> One of these officers, named Alexander, who was a young civil engineer in peace-time, became so completely wrapped up in the elephants and oozies working under him that he learned all their names in a week, and struggled hard to learn Burmese, bribing the oozies with cigarettes to give him lessons in the evenings. All was going well when a sudden disaster occurred. Okethapyah (Pagoda Stone), one of his best animals, was blown up by a Mark 5 land-mine near his camp. Alexander came rushing over a most fearsome track in a jeep, arriving at two a.m., to tell me all about it. He said its back legs had been flown off, but he had seen it move, and was afraid it might be still alive! The Burmans who came with him assured me in

Map of North-West Burma, showing the route of the party of forty-five elephants, forty irregular Karens, ninety elephant riders and attendants, sixty-four women and children, and four officers in April 1944, to Imphal and Baladan in Assam. (From Lieutenant-Colonel J. H. Williams, *Elephant Bill*, (London, 1952))

Burmese that the animal was stone dead. I gave Alex a good tot of rum, and told him I could not amputate an elephant's legs, and we could only do our best to prevent such accidents in future. He abandoned the subject, but asked me to give him a lesson in Burmese—at two-thirty a.m.! I went back with him, starting before dawn, taking an anti-tank rifle, in case he had been right; but of course the elephant was dead—a sad sight in the early morning hours. The men had already discovered three more Mark 5 land-mines, and led us to them.

I knew that they had been put down by a British infantry battalion six months before, during the retreat, and never mapped. Having been exposed all through the monsoon rains, they were most uncertain things to handle. However, Alex, being a sapper officer, considered it to be his duty to pick them up there and then, and replace the safety-pins. He told me to take the Burmans away behind trees while he was doing this. Two of the men, however, flatly refused, saying that if Thakin (Alex) wasn't afraid, they weren't, and anyhow they wanted to see just how it was done. So we all stayed and watched. While Alex removed the claw-clamp and the lid, he asked me to explain the sheer wire and how the pin had to be replaced. 'Simple enough!' exclaimed Tun Myin, one of the Burmans who was watching. And next morning he brought in five more land-mines all with their safety-pins replaced, just as Alex had done them.

When Alex was not at hand I always felt that, but for the Grace of God, there goes Elephant Bill!

By December 1944 four roads were fit for transport to the River Chindwin:

Tamu to Tonhe in the north
Tamu to Sittang in the east
Tamu to Yuwa in the east
Tamu to Kalewa to the south.

Two hundred and seventy log bridges had been put in by the elephants allowing motor transport and tanks to move forward. The final job was to lay a bridge over the Neyinzaya River for the tanks engaged in taking Kalemyo.

During the war elephants had many jobs to undertake, which they had never encountered in peacetime. When assisting in bridge construction they frequently had to lift logs up to a height of 10 feet, from ground level to bridge level, which weighed on average a quarter of a ton each, and were often too heavy for the elephant's trunk to hold. So they learnt to balance them on the tusks, but this was dangerous for the oozie sitting on the elephant's neck. So the elephants learnt to jam a stout piece of wood between trunk and tusk to act as a vertical stop to prevent the big log rolling back over his forehead onto his rider. 'Elephant Bill' gives numerous other examples of the elephant's intelligence in his book.

As the Allies pushed southwards more elephants were found, made fit for service, and used on road construction on the line of advance south from Kalemyo to Gangaw, up the valley of the Myittha River and over towards Meiktila. During the Allied advance south elephants were needed more than ever, mostly for bridge building, but also for releasing vehicles bogged down in the monsoon mud. It was, said 'Elephant Bill', just as though they were drawing corks out of champagne bottles. Throughout the conflict elephants proved themselves to be adaptable and

The first bridge constructed by elephants for the XIVth Army, over the Lokechao Creek. (From Lieutenant-Colonel J. H. Williams, *Elephant Bill*, (London, 1952))

intelligent, working calmly alongside heavy machinery and loyally obedient to their oozies. The oozie and his elephant had to act as one, and 'Elephant Bill' exercised great skill in selecting and training his oozies and then matching them to the elephants. Through his time with 'Elephant Bill' John Alexander gained a great and lasting respect and love for these giants of the forest, which he carried with him for the rest of his life.

The British Commander and Indian crew of a Sherman tank of the 9th Royal Deccan Horse, 255th Indian Tank Brigade, meet a newly liberated elephant on the road to Meiktila, 29 March 1945. (© Imperial War Museum)

Object: 17. Photo of Elephant and Rider.

17. THE ELEPHANT BANDOOLA

Strictly speaking, this is not one of the objects that John Alexander brought home with him! But he did return home from Burma with a deep love of and respect for the elephants that were used by the Royal Engineers to help build bridges and roads. The most remarkable of these animals was an elephant called Bandoola, named in honour of the legendary Burmese General Maha Bandoola who commanded the armed forces from 1821 until his death in 1825 fighting against the British.

Elephants and human beings live about as long as each other, and can therefore acquire a lifelong mutual knowledge of each other's characters. Lieutenant-General J. H. Williams, 'Elephant Bill', and Bandoola were born on roughly the same date in 1897, and Williams in his work with the elephants in Burma quickly established a rapport with this impressive animal who stood more than 9 feet high, with lavender skin and pink freckles across his cheeks and with huge tusks.

In a book he wrote in 1953 J. H. Williams gave a separate account of Bandoola and his life-long relationship with his *oozie* Po Toke, who was determined to train Bandoola by

kindness rather than by breaking his spirit, which was the usual method. When he was taken onto the logging strength of the Bombay Burma Trading Corporation Bandoola was described as follows:

Name	Sex	Born	Mother
Bandoola	Male	Nov. 1897	Ma Shwe

Height	7ft. 4 in.
Tusks	Swai Gah. *Right*, 2 ft. *Left*, 2 ft. 0½ in.
Feet	Perfect. *Toes: Fore*, 10. *Hind*, 8.
Back	Banana Leaf.
Tail	To hock. *Brush*: Good, few white hairs.
Ears	Good, heavy-haired in orifice.
Skin	Loose and heavily corrugated.
Eyes	Pearly ring around parrot bead.
Brands	"C" on both rumps.
Identification Scars	Nil.
Remarks	Purchased from U. Ohn Ghine, Contractor, as trained calf, aged six. Trained by Maung Po Toke. Good temper.

Williams describes the particular challenges, frustrations and enjoyment of working with these highly intelligent but unpredictable animals, until he had to leave the northern regions of Burma in 1935. He didn't see Bandoola or Po Toke again for seven years, by which time the Japanese army was flooding into Burma, and the Allies were in retreat. Bandoola was busy building bridges for the retreating army, and J. H. Williams told Po Toke to take him away and hide him from the Japanese. Po Toke made for his native village of Witok in the Kabaw Valley and concealed Bandoola in the jungle, but he was always fearful that he would be discovered by a Japanese or Allied patrol and shot. However, in October 1942, during a break in the monsoon rains, Po Toke was contacted and told to bring Bandoola to J. H. Williams, who was in camp at Tamu. Bandoola was handed over to Williams in November to become No. 1 War Elephant in his Elephant Company, the first of the elephants to fight for the freedom of Burma from the Japanese. When Williams undertook the daunting task of taking his Elephant Company over the hills into India to escape from the Japanese, it was Bandoola who led the party. When at one point they came to an almost sheer cliff, Bandoola led the elephants up the steps which they cut in the rock and along a narrow path with a sheer precipice on one side. Williams called it 'a moment of greatness' and declared, 'Without Bandoola and Po Toke we should never have come through, the whole company of forty-five elephants, forty armed Karens, the ninety elephant riders and attendants, the sixty-four refugee women and children and the four officers' (J. H. Williams, *Bandoola* (London, 1953), p. 240).

Thanks to this extraordinary combination of animal-human relationship and co-operation the entire party reached the safety of James Sinclair's tea plantation at Baledan in Assam.

It was Bandoola, too, who led the group of elephants back into Burma in November 1944, with his *oozie* Po Toke guiding him. *Oozie* is the Burmese word for *mahout*, which is a Hindi word meaning an elephant handler and keeper. From January to March 1945 Bandoola was attached to saw-mill units and the shipyard at Kalewa, which were building boats for the army. When Williams arrived at the camp Bandoola had gone missing and sadly he was eventually found shot dead on 8 March with his right tusk missing. His death was a mystery, but he remained a hero to John Alexander, who for the rest of his life retained a love of elephants born of his experiences in the Burma Campaign.

Chapter VIII

Advance to Victory

With the defeat of the main Japanese divisions in the campaigns of 1944, the Allied High Command realised that the reconquest of Burma was now a practical proposition. Throughout the monsoon of 1944 thousands of British, Indian and African troops of the XIVth Army, backed up by British, Chinese and American troops in the north, pushed steadily south to establish positions from which the final assault could be launched.

> Across the hills, down the valleys, the Japanese Army, broken but always ready to stand and fight a rearguard action, was streaming. Diseased, hungry, they were short of everything, it seemed, except ammunition. They were pursued through Tiddim, and although they made a stand at the 'Chocolate Staircase' and Kennedy Peak, eventually the Allies pushed on to Kalemyo, reached Kalewa and established a solid bridgehead on the east bank of the Chindwin River. On the left flank the 19th Indian Division pushed across the river to link up with the 2nd Division's advance at Schwebo. General Slim realised that the Japanese were not going to remain in the Schwebo Plain, and issued orders for 'Operation Extended Capital', an ambitious deception plan and flanking manouvre. Thus 33 Corps continued to advance in the centre on Schwebo. However 4 Corps, instead of attacking Mandalay from the north-west, would conduct a covert move south, over the lines of 33 Corps, and would suddenly appear at Pakokku, seize a crossing, and without pause strike violently with armoured and airborne forces at Meiktila. (General Slim, *Defeat into Victory* (London Cassell, 1956), p. 393)

Slim knew that the Japanese were expecting him to attack at Mandalay. By a surprise attack on Meiktila, a lightly defended but essential supply base 100 miles to the south, Slim hoped to catch them unawares and undermine the defence of Mandalay. (See *The 14th Army in Burma: A Case Study in Delivering Fighting Power*: Major R. M. Borton: *Defense Studies*: Vol. 2: No. 3. Autumn 2002, p. 37).

On 2 February 1945 the 17th Indian Division commenced a three-pronged attack to the south from Imphal. 63 Brigade were to advance to Tiddim and Fort White to capture Falam, and then move forwards to Pakokku and Meiktila. The 48 Brigade were to take the central route via Palel, Sittaung, Kalewa and Schwebo to Mandalay, and 99 Brigade were to head south-east to the Shan States. As the advance had started one month before the end of the monsoon season the Japanese were taken by surprise, and 63 Brigade made rapid progress thanks to the work of the sappers of 60 Field Company. The entire 63 Brigade crossed the Chindwin River, transported by 60 Field Company under fire using Bailey pontoons powered by outboard motors, and in similar fashion

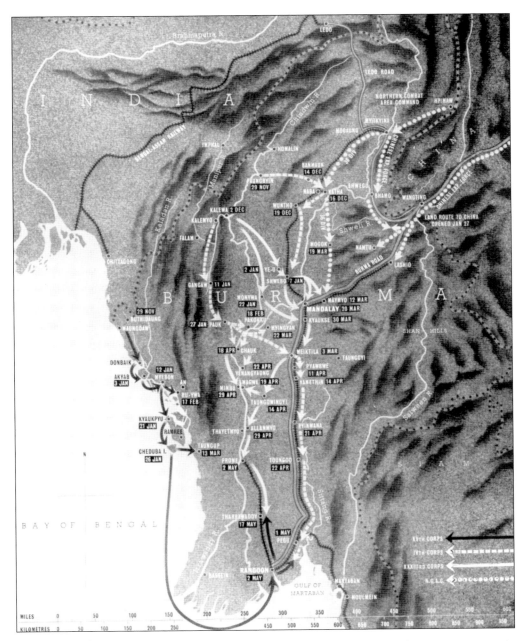

The reconquest of Burma. In December 1944 four armies went on the offensive: XV Corps in Arakan, IV and XXXIII Corps in the central area, and the Northern Combat Area Command from the north. The battles between the Chindwin and Mandalay were hard fought, but General Slim crossed the Irrawaddy at Pakokku, took Meiktila and Mandalay, switching the XXXIII Corps into the Yenangyaung oilfields and the IV over to the Pegu Road. The amphibious assaults down the Arakan coast secured airfields that covered and supplied the southern front, and then XV Corps sailed for Rangoon and took it from the sea. (HMSO, 1946)

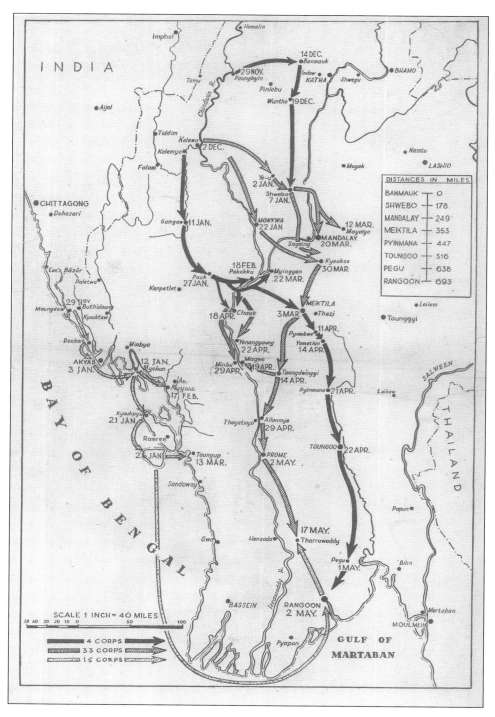

Map showing the routes taken by the Allies as they advanced from Kalewa at the beginning of 1945. (From *S.E.A.C. Souvenir Newspaper*, November 1944)

Above left: A lorry of the 36th Infantry Division enters the town of Tigyiang during the advance down the Irrawaddy towards Mandalay, 22 December 1944. (© Imperial War Museum)

Above right: The railway system was used extensively both by the Japanese and the Allies for supply purposes. During the Allied advance south a Bristol Beaufighter of No. 27 Squadron RAF makes an attack on Japanese goods wagons on the railway line between Monywa and Sagaing in Central Burma. (© Imperial War Museum)

the Irrawaddy River was crossed. The move south to the Irrawaddy was remarkable for the few vehicle casualties incurred over 400 miles of terrible roads. On 18 February Meiktila Force, consisting of the 17th Indian Division and the 255 Indian Tank Brigade, started to cross the Irrawaddy near Pagan. As they crossed the soldiers would have gazed on the impressive city of Pagan, the ancient capital of Burma, destroyed by Kublai Khan, deserted now except for the ruins of 5,000 pagodas. By 21 February the crossing was completed, and the vast concourse of tanks, artillery, armoured cars, and infantry deployed over the plain, moving east towards Meiktila, only 80 miles ahead. By

Amid the brutalities of the battlefield, it was sometimes possible to encounter humanity and kindness too.

Squadron Leader Joseph Heaven, an RAF Methodist chaplain, plays with a Burmese baby in a village near Monywa, March 1945, where he found forty Burmese Christians who had been evacuated from the Methodist Mission Compound and School at Monywa. (© Imperial War Museum)

March the force had battered its way through enemy opposition over little more than bullock cart tracks, captured many dumps, and were now concentrated on the attack on Meiktila, a garrison town of over 2,000 Japanese soldiers.

The 17th Indian Division under Major-General 'Punch' Cowan sailed from Nyaungu bridgehead and reached Taungtha by 24 February. While 63 Brigade proceeded on foot to establish a roadblock south-west of Meiktila to prevent Japanese reinforcements reaching the garrison, the main body of the division, including the 48th Indian Infantry Brigade and 255 Indian Tank Brigade, attacked the town from the west.

It took four days to capture the town. The entire 17th Division including 48 Brigade, 63 Brigade, 60 Field Company and 255 Tank Brigade were concentrated on the attack. The tanks of 255 Brigade and the infantry worked in tandem, and the Engineers were removing mines with the forward troops. Yard by yard the town was taken and held. The Japanese fought fanatically and every one of them died where he stood. They squatted in bunkers with mines between their legs and holding a brick to detonate them when the tanks rolled over them. In four days over 2,000 were killed and fifty-six guns destroyed or captured. Meiktila with its airstrip and the surrounding area was finally secured on 5 March 1945.

The capture of Meiktila was the greatest defeat the Japanese had suffered in South-East Asia Command. It was a vital communications hub for the Japanese 15th Army and its loss handicapped their operations in the Mandalay area. Although they counterattacked strongly, shelling the airstrip so that supplies had to be delivered by airdrop, Allied tank and artillery columns constantly pushed out from Meiktila in all directions, and by the end of March the Japanese were broken. They had lost 90 per cent of their artillery, and 4,000 soldiers and seventy guns had been destroyed or captured.

Above left: The attack on Mandalay, February–March 1945. Men of a Sikh Regiment clear a Japanese foxhole at Mandalay with a bayonet charge after throwing in a phosphorus grenade. (© Imperial War Museum)

Above right: The Capture of Mandalay February–March 1945. Men of the Madras Sappers stand at the gates of Fort Dufferin at Mandalay after the Japanese had fled. (© Imperial War Museum)

Meanwhile as part of 'Operation Extended Capital', 33 Corps moved swiftly towards Schwebo and Monywa on their way to Mandalay, while to the west 15 Corps pressed forward in Arakan taking Akyab and Ramree by coastal assault so that the airfields could supply the XIVth Army. At the same time the Northern Combat Area Command struck down from the north, moving towards Lashio and the Burma Road. General Slim's plan had come together. He had crossed the Irrawaddy at Pakokku, caught the Japanese by surprise, taken Meiktila and then Mandalay.

The Meiktila Force moved south towards Pyawbwe on 3 April, meeting strong opposition. Villages that had supported Japanese troops were set on fire, and about 400 Japanese were killed. The advance towards Pyawbwe was three-pronged. 63 Brigade advanced along the western flank following the Japanese withdrawal south. 48 Brigade advanced in the centre along the main road, and 99 Brigade moved south along the line of the railway. Pyawbwe was captured after fierce resistance, on 10 April, and over 1,100 Japanese soldiers were killed. This victory completed the Japanese disorganisation begun at Meiktila. From there on the advance south was largely a pursuit. The 5th Division leapfrogged the 17th to march south and occupy Toungoo, while 63 Brigade advanced along the main road towards Pegu. The Allies were simply too strong and too swift for the Japanese to offer much resistance, although fierce fighting took place in isolated pockets. 63 Brigade with 60 Field Company sent many patrols out to hold bridges and clear the area of mines and booby traps.

Pegu was a hard nut to crack, but it was eventually taken by determined attacks from the north, east and west. Early monsoon rains added to the difficulties, and washed away two bridges between Pegu and Rangoon, so the rapid advance of the 17th Indian Division was slowed down. 60 Field Company was kept busy erecting Bailey Bridges, and as the division advanced further bridges were built to replace those destroyed by the retreating Japanese troops. On 6 May the 17th Indian Division made contact with the 1st Lincolns of the 71st Indian Infantry Brigade at the Hlegu bridgehead, where the pontoon bridge that had been washed away was replaced with a new bridge. While the 17th Indian Division was ordered to remain in the area of Pegu to perform mopping-up operations, the 26th Division took over the advance and drove south to Rangoon as John Masters, in *The Road Past Mandalay* (Michael Joseph, 1963, p. 303) describes:

> The dust thickened under the trees lining the road until the column was motoring into a thunderous yellow tunnel, first the tanks, infantry all over them, then trucks filled with men, then more tanks, going fast, nose to tail, guns, more trucks, more guns – British, Sikhs, Gurkhas, Madrassis, Pathans … All these men knew their commanders and as the vehicles crashed past most of the soldiers were on their feet cheering and yelling.
>
> … The romance of war – but only a fool would grudge us the excitement and sense of glory, for no one on that plain had wanted war, and all of us had known enough horror to last several lifetimes.
>
> This was the old Indian Army going down to the attack, for the last time in its history, exactly two hundred and fifty years after the Honourable East India Company had enlisted its first ten sepoys on the Coromandel Coast.

During the prolonged campaign, and the push southwards, covering 725 miles from Imphal to Hlegu in three months, the Japanese army had suffered massive casualties, over 10,000 killed, 167 captured, and 212 guns and fifteen tanks taken. On 6 May the

Above left: An American photographer surrounded by discarded and worthless paper money on the streets of Rangoon, May 1945. (Wikipedia Commons)

Above right: Even amid the demands of war soldiers could find the time to appreciate the beauty of the country in which they were fighting. Off-duty soldiers enjoying the sights of Rangoon's pagodas, 13 May 1945. (© Imperial War Museum)

17th Division proudly put up their 'Black Cat' sign again. With the decisive defeat of the Japanese 33rd Army 'The Black Cats' could feel that they had avenged the losses sustained since 1942. On 3 May 1945 the 26th Division had occupied Rangoon from the sea against very light opposition and made contact with the 17th Division south of Pegu, but a further advance was hampered by a shortage of supplies and worsening weather conditions. The task of 17 Division was now to mop up enemy units attempting to escape east across the Sittang River. During the 'Battle of the Breakout' Cowan's 17th Division slaughtered the Japanese 55th Division on the banks of the Sittang, upstream from the spot where two thirds of the division had been left behind three years before. The humiliation of the long retreat of 1942 had at last been avenged.

Lieutenant General Takenhara, commander of Japanese 49th Division, hands his sword to Major General Arthur Crowther DSO, commander of the 17th Indian Division, at Thaton, north of Moulmein, Burma. (© Imperial War Museum)

Object: 18. Japanese Currency.

18. JAPANESE INVASION MONEY

These banknotes, officially known as Southern Regions Development Banknotes, were the currency issued by the Japanese military authorities as a replacement for the local currency after the conquest of Burma in 1942. The Southern Regions Development Bank provided financial services in areas of South-East Asia occupied by the Japanese forces. All notes bore the name of the Imperial Japanese Government and were printed in Tokyo.

In Burma they issued paper currency of 1, 5 and 10 cents, and ¼, ½, 1, 5 and 10 Rupees. In 1944 a 100 Rupee note was issued. The Japanese characters in the oblong box at the bottom of each note read 'Government of Imperial Japan', and the seal at the lower left side shows the symbol for the Minister of Finance. The Burma series of notes are also stamped with the code 'B' in red. The Rupee notes include an image of the Ananda Temple at Pagan, a Buddhist temple built in AD 1100, which has been called 'the Westminster Abbey of Burma'. The Allies began making counterfeit copies of these notes to try to undermine the currency, which, in any case, after the defeat of the Japanese, was rendered completely worthless. Japanese troops were ordered to destroy bank records and any remaining currency prior to capitulation, but many millions of notes remained in circulation.

Tons of notes were burned, and Allied forces took samples of the currency as souvenirs at the end of the campaign, as they lay discarded in their thousands in the towns that the Japanese had abandoned in their retreat.

Dimensions:
Half Rupee note BD 12 cm x 5.75 cm.

Quarter Rupee BC
Ten Cents BF 5 cm x 10.5 cm.
Ten Cents <u>M</u>
      AN

Five Cents BE 10 cm x 4.75 cm.
One Cent <u>M</u> 9.5 cm x 4.5 cm.
      AD

Chapter IX

From Sapper to Civilian

On 7 May 1945 John Alexander was posted to take command of 65 Field Company in 62 Brigade of 19 Division, based at Taunggyi in the Shan Hills. Situated at an elevation of just under 5,000 feet, Taunggyi was at the time a delightful hill station with its own colonial governor and garrison. John gained some much-needed rest, but his main task was to reconstruct the Taunggyi-Kentung road, so opening up the trade route into China, and to make operational the branch line from Meiktila to Taunggyi. The other objectives of 19 Division were to prevent a Japanese breakout from Pegu Yomas, and to engage with the 17th Division in general mopping-up operations east of the Sittang River.

Major John Willis Alexander with 65 Company, QVO Madras Sappers and Miners, Taunggyi, 1945. (Author's collection)

65 Company Headquarters, Taunggyi, Shan States. (Author's collection)

Takaw Bridge, constructed by 65 Field Company in 1945. A bridge on the road from Thazi, east of Meiktila, which crossed the Salween River at Takaw, previously served by a wire-held ferry of only one 3-ton lorry capacity. The ferry point was in a gorge 800 feet above sea level and surrounded by 7,000-feet-high mountains. (Author's collection)

John was proud to record that the road was completed, and the railway line made operational, in just three months.

By August 1945 the Japanese High Command made contact with the 17th Indian Division to sue for surrender. For Lieutenant Shuichiro Yoshimo, of the 11th Epidemic Prevention and Water Supply Unit, 18th Division, and many other Japanese soldiers, the war ended on 15 August 1945. He was labelled 'Japanese Surrendered Personnel' and put in a concentration camp. While there he remembered a visitor arriving:

> One day a brigade commander of 'The Black Cats' (17 Indian Division) came to our camp. We assembled and listened to him. He said: 'You have become prisoners as you have been defeated in war. Don't hang your heads; you stopped fighting by order of the Emperor. I know from my experience of fighting with you that you Japanese have great ability. I believe that you are sure to make Japan a first-rate country after you have returned to your home country. Be confident and behave yourselves so that you can get home without trouble.'
>
> The speech was a great encouragement to us. We left Rangoon on 13th June 1946 by the US ship 'Whitehead' and landed in Japan on 10th July. My parents were so happy to see me.
> (Kazuo Tamayama and John Nunneley, *Tales by Japanese Soldiers* (Weidenfeld and Nicholson 1992))

The Surrender Ceremony of the Japanese Forces at Rangoon, 28 August 1945. General Numata Takazo signs the surrender agreement. (© Imperial War Museum)

Japanese prisoners from the Penwegon area (on railway line near Sittang River, north of Rangoon) are searched, 30 July 1945. (© Imperial War Museum)

After the reconquest of Thailand, Malaya and Singapore, the final act of total surrender took place on 12 September 1945 in the impressive Council Chamber of Singapore's Municipal Buildings, where General Itagaki, Japanese Commander in Malaya, Sumatra and Java, signed the surrender of all the Japanese armed forces in South-East Asia, numbering 650,000 men. Accompanied by his fellow Commanders, Supreme Allied Commander SEAC, Admiral Lord Louis Mountbatten accepted their surrender, the death-knell of Japanese militaristic ambitions in Asia.

The Allied XIVth Army was finally disbanded on 1 December 1945. General Sir William Slim, Commander-in-Chief Land Forces, South-East Asia, told his troops in an order of the day:

> When you were first formed, I told you that you could become one of the best-known armies that the British Empire ever had. And so you did. Inheriting a legacy of defeat and disaster, constantly short of equipment and men you, by your discipline, your stubborn courage, your skill, and above all by your refusal to be beaten by men or nature, achieved a success few thought possible. Many races fighting and working in the comradeship of the Fourteenth Army learnt to appreciate one another's value. Carry that mutual respect into the future, wherever you may be called. Carry with you, too, those qualities that made the Fourteenth Army what it was. Whether you serve on or return to civil life, they will be required, and the world will be a better place because you have retained them.

As John Alexander came towards the end of his time as a member of that vast XIVth Army, and began planning his return to civilian life, he may well have reflected how he, an ordinary person had come to be mixed up in this bitter and prolonged struggle. What was he doing in Burma, thousands of miles from home, hunting Japanese soldiers

Field Marshall Sir William Slim (1891–1970). GOC XIVth Army, standing outside XIVth Army Headquarters in Burma, 5 March 1945. (© Imperial War Museum)

who were themselves thousands of miles from their homes? He along with most of his comrades in arms had joined up to protect his country and do his duty, perhaps imbued with the belief that the British Empire was the greatest force for good that the world had ever known. If they expected gratitude from the Burmese population, they were soon painfully surprised to find themselves barely tolerated. John had been trained as a soldier and an engineer, and he went where he was deployed, to fight an enemy whom he came to believe was brutal, insensitive and fanatical. For nearly four years in the jungles of Burma he had lived on soy link sausages, bully beef, and dehydrated vegetables, drinking water that was always chlorinated and tasted like rotten eggs, smoking cigarettes that tasted worse than tarred rope, suffering flies, mosquitos, dhobi rash, jungle sores and malaria, scorched by the tropical sun and lashed by the monsoon rains. Being shelled, mortared and continually shot at by the invisible Japanese wore all his finer feelings threadbare, until the growing impulse to kill took control of heart, brain and trigger finger. To John Alexander and most of his fellow soldiers the Japanese were a strange and alien people. The Allies had been told many wartime stories of their savage behaviour, so that while they admired Japanese courage and endurance, it was easier and safer to think of them as dangerous animals. General Bill Slim summed up the prevailing view:

The Japanese soldier was a brutalised creature: a killer of wounded: a torturer. The Japanese was a ravager of women: a looter: a liar. He had to be driven out of Burma for the sake of the people of that land, who otherwise would have dwelt in a night of savagery.

90

Although frontline rations were spartan, the army found resourceful ways to keep the troops fed and watered.

Two cooks at an RAF motor transport repair unit in Central Burma take a morning break in front of their two stoves, made from salvaged petrol cans and ammunition boxes. On the left is Corporal W. Tennery from Penzance, and on right is Corporal G. W. Fountain of Leighton Buzzard, Bedfordshire. (© Imperial War Museum)

In that context it was easy to believe that 'The only good Jap is a dead one'. So the Allies became as ruthless in the jungle as their enemy, and tended to follow the principle quoted by General Bill Slim: 'There's only one principle of war, and that's this. Hit the other fellow, as quick as you can, and as hard as you can, where it hurts him most, when he aint looking!' Or as John Alexander put it with considerable understatement:'It was either you or them. You were fighting not only against the Japs, but also against the jungle and the monsoon. It wasn't a very pleasant place to have a war.'

It has been said that the Burma Campaign had all the elements of a great Homeric saga.

It took place in a fantastic terrain, isolated by great mountains and jungles from any other theatre. It went on unbroken for three years and eight months. It covered vast areas. It sucked into its maelstrom nearly 2,000,000 men. It encompassed great disasters and ended in great triumphs. It produced prodigies of heroism, patience, resolution and endurance. It brought about great suffering, but fascinated and enthralled those taking part in it, both victors and losers. It was like no war that had ever been in the history of conflict.

(Arthur Swinson in *Purnell's Illustrated History of the Second World War*)

91

What sustained so many soldiers was the thought of their loved ones back home. Geoffrey Hayward carried this photograph of his mother, with the inscription on the back: 'Here's Mum waiting for your return at the front door, so please hurry! November 22nd 1942.' Three years later Geoffrey finally arrived home. (Chris Pearce)

For nearly four long years John Alexander had played his part in this Homeric saga. He had stayed on to assist in the reconstruction of the country's communications by rebuilding the Taunggyi–Kentung road and opening up the railway from Meiktila to Taunggyi. Throughout the campaign he had been sustained by his love for Audrey Harker, the girl whom he had met at a dance at Aldershot Barracks five years previously, and to whom he had become engaged when on leave in 1944. They corresponded regularly, Audrey sending him news of home and assurances of her love, and John reciprocating with saucy home-made postcards full of typical forces humour, which must have raised an eyebrow when shown to her parents! John came home before his division was officially disbanded, frustrated that having been made up to the rank of major, he had to revert to the rank of Captain, but elated at the prospect of being reunited with Audrey and getting married. He arrived back in England in June 1946 and five days later the marriage took place! He received his demobilisation papers in August, and returned to his studies at King's College, Cambridge. After graduating in 1948 he pursued a successful and fulfilling career as a civil engineer, travelling all over the world on engineering projects. But the scars of his wartime experiences remained, along with his eclectic collection of souvenirs, a mute reminder of battles fought in the exotic but terrifying jungles of Burma, to which he never returned except in his recurring nightmares.

Objects: 19. Saucy Postcards, 20. Sapphire Rings.

19. POSTCARDS HOME

During the Second World War servicemen could send postcards home without paying postage. They became an easy and important way for soldiers to keep in touch with their families, wives and girlfriends back home, a quick means of letting them know that 'I'm still alive and thinking about you'. Some were patriotic, some were humorous and some were mildly risqué.

   These examples from a series of homemade service postcards were sent by the then Lieutenant J. W. Alexander to his fiancée Audrey Harker during February 1945. Entitled 'Crazy Cartoons', they are crudely drawn but saucy, typical of service humour and must have made Audrey smile.

Dimensions: 14 cm x 10 cm

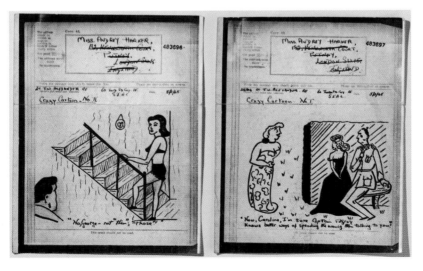

Chapter X

Not Forgotten

One of the reasons why the soldiers of the Burma Campaign were known as the 'Forgotten Army' is that the XIVth Army was largely an Asian army. At the start of the campaign an Indian brigade comprised one British battalion and two Indian battalions, but General Slim altered this system so that brigades were either all British or all Indian, because he felt that the soldiers fought better that way. Slim believed implicitly in the fighting qualities and dogged endurance of his troops:

> My Indian divisions after 1943 were among the best in the world. They would go anywhere, do anything, go on doing it, and do it on very little.
> (*Defeat into Victory* (London: 1956), p. 539)

As Colonel John Masters reflected:

> As the tanks burst away down the road to Rangoon ... they took possession of the empire we had built ... Twenty races, a dozen religions, a score of languages passed in those trucks and tanks. When my great-great-grandfather first went to India there had been as many nations: now there was one – India.
> (*The Road Past Mandalay*, pp. 312–13)

The seeds of the rise of India to become in the late 20th century an independent nation and an emerging global power were first sown during the Second World War, 'when a desperately poor country mobilized to an astonishing degree and simultaneously fought for its own freedom and that of the world'. (Srinath Raghavan, *India's War* (Penguin Books, 2017), p. 6)

To General Slim belongs the achievement of building up the management and morale of this multi-ethnic army from the despair and disillusion of 1942. The regimental system helped to build and improve morale and a fighting spirit, and here the divisions were key to success, the 'ball of fire' of the 5th Indian Division, the 'dagger' of the 19th Indian Division, and the 'black cat' of the 17th Indian Division, whose fortunes have formed the thread running through this account of the Burma Campaign. It was their spirit of endurance, personified in the experiences of Captain John Alexander, that saw the division, and the whole XIVth Army, through its painful transition from demoralised retreat to eventual victory.

John Alexander was one of the lucky ones who survived the war, and who came home to a new life in post-war England. Many did not come back. During the long advance from the Irrawaddy to Pegu, the 17th Division alone had 719 men killed,

2,767 wounded, and seventy-one missing. Official casualty figures for Allied land forces in Burma came to more than 14,000 killed, 44,731 wounded, and 14,552 missing. But the Japanese lost 190,000 men killed in Burma, three-fifths of those who were sent out to fight, including Second Lieutenant Shoichi Yoshida, whose 'Good Luck' flags John Alexander brought home in his collection of war souvenirs.

For those who did not return home the words on the famous Kohima memorial are an appropriate epitaph. The memorial itself is a large monolith of Naga stone dedicated to the 2nd British Division and standing in the cemetery of Kohima in the far north-east of India. On a pedestal stands a small cross, and below it is set a bronze panel with the inscription:

When You Go Home, Tell Them Of Us And Say,
For Your Tomorrow, We Gave Our Today.

The words owe their origin to the ancient Greek poet Simonides of Kios (586–468 BC), who wrote of the Spartans holding the pass at Thermopylae against Xerxes and the Persian Army in 480 BC:

O Stranger, go home and tell the Spartans that we lie here in obedience to their orders.

The words on the monument were an imperfectly remembered version of the lines written by John Maxwell Edmonds, a classical scholar, at the suggestion of Major John Etty-Leal of the 2nd Division. In the beautiful and serene surroundings of the Kohima cemetery this simple memorial sums up the heroism and sacrifice of those who fought in a far-off land, and the debt we owe them.

Above: The design for the memorial of the 2nd British Division at Kohima. Two hundred Naga tribesmen brought the memorial stone from the hills and placed it in position as their tribute to those who had died. (From *S.E.A.C. Souvenir Newspaper*, November 1944)

Right: Two soldiers visit the Military Cemetery at Kohima to see the grave of their comrade Lance-Corporal John Harman VC, who was awarded the Victoria Cross posthumously for gallantry at Kohima, 8–9 April 1944. (© Imperial War Museum)

20. BURMESE SAPPHIRE RINGS

As John and Audrey Harker picked up the threads of their life together and prepared to get married in the summer of 1946, they would doubtless have reflected on their years apart, on how the war had stolen from them and so many others the simple ordinary joys of a young couple shaping a shared life. They had known the agony of separation, and the too rare, too short, joys of reunion. Apart they had endured illness, danger and fears for each other. They had been separated for four years, and now had to learn to live together, overcoming the barriers set up by experiences that had not been shared. Behind them, as they began married life, would have flitted the shadows of those they had known who had not survived, colleagues of Audrey's from the WRNS killed by flying bombs, fellow soldiers in John's brigade who were cut down in the jungles of Burma, or who succumbed to malaria or dysentery. They were all so young. Shadows which sadly faded as the years went by, those who could never now share in the joys and hopes of this young couple, whose lives lay before them in a world of peace.

When he came home John Alexander brought with him a small collection of Burmese sapphires and a small gold ring with three sapphires set in a row. Sapphire is one of the two gem varieties of corundum, the other being ruby, and both are found in Burma's Mogok Stone Tract, which lies 200 kilometres north-east of Mandalay. Sapphires from this area display an intense royal blue colour and great clarity. Burmese sapphires are considered relatively young compared to deposits in parts of Africa, but that still means that they date back to between 450 and 750 million years ago.

Precious stones have always been symbols of love, and John must have thought of that when he met a Burmese princess during his time in Burma. She was a descendant of the last King of Burma, King Thibaw, exiled by the British in 1885. She gave John his small collection of sapphires and a ring, which he brought home to give to his 'darling Audrey', a token of the love that had kept him going, and kept him sane, during the gruelling years of the Burma campaign. Sapphires in particular are associated with romantic love, representing fidelity and romantic devotion. So it is appropriate that the last of this collection of twenty objects is this sapphire ring which Audrey treasured all her life, and which on her death passed to her daughter, who, on her engagement, had two of the sapphires from John's collection incorporated in her own engagement ring. These rings remain both a reminder of the land in which John served as a soldier, and a symbol of the love which sustained them both, and which ultimately is more enduring than the hatreds of war.